The Lost Chapters of Humanity on Earth

Anastasia Martin

HISTORIUM
BOOKS

Copyright © 2024 by Anastasia Martin

This is a work of nonfiction.

No part of this publication may be reproduced, distributed, or transmitted in any form, or by any means, including photocopying, screenshots, recording, or other electronic or mechanical methods, without the prior written permission of the publisher, except in the case of brief quotations embodied in reviews and certain other non-commercial uses permitted by copyright law.

Cover design by White Rabbit Arts

Follow the author at
www. thehistoricalfictioncompany. com/hp-authors/anastasia-martin

EBOOK ISBN: 979-8-9883817-8-5
PAPERBACK ISBN: 978-1-962465-46-5
HARDCOVER ISBN: 978-1-962465-53-3

Published by Historium Press 2024
New York, NY / Macon, GA USA

This book is being published with special thanks to my high school English and Drama teacher, Darren Ralston, without whom I may never have published. After having been discouraged by so many influential adults in my life telling me my writing was nonsense and too bizarre for anyone else to want to read, Mr. Ralston saw it as unique and refreshing. He supported and encouraged the idea of me becoming a published author.

Special thanks, also, to Professor William Munsey for believing in me and reinspiring my imagination by giving me a new appreciation for Chemistry. Also, for indulging my two-and half-hour tour down the science fiction rabbit holes of potential organo-metallic robotic life forms and non-carbon-based life forms existing elsewhere in the Universe.

More thanks to school cafeteria workers everywhere. I don't know if I would be alive today were it not for the kindness of those who recognized a child going without and risked their jobs to give me what they could. I don't know whether they knew I was taking it home to feed my younger siblings or simply saw a hungry child. To every underappreciated cafeteria worker who feels unnoticed, you are the unseen superheroes. I promise it matters more than you may realize.

Table of Contents

Section One

Genetic Memory

Have you ever remembered something that didn't happen? Have you ever known something you shouldn't have? Many believe these phenomena to be something akin to the sensation known as Déjà vu. However, some attribute them to genetic memory. The theory of Genetic Memory proposes that information, such as past knowledge and experiences, can be passed on to future generations through DNA. I fully subscribe to this theory because I first started asking about Genetic Memory when I was three years old, not by name of course, but rather by definition. I dreamt about things I could never have known or had the opportunity to be exposed to at any point. Then I later found those things to be factual.

Could genetic memory be a contributor to evolution and explain why there seems to be a large amount of our brain that we don't use? Could we be using it as storage? Maybe we really do know all the answers and are just unable to consciously recall them. Genetic memory may also provide some insight into what we dream and why. Our ancestors may have given us all the explanations we seek. Where did we come from? How did we become humanity as we know it today? Sometimes I think those answers come to us in the form of inspiration for the astonishing and fantastical stories we conceive.

Where do ideas come from? Where does consciousness come from, and for that matter, subconsciousness? When I was four, I had a dream about a large, brilliant red bird that when it flew seemed to be aflame. In my dream I told my twin brother about it, and he said the bird was called Phoenix. When I woke, I remembered the dream so clearly because I was truly enthralled by the bird I had seen. About a year later I came across a phoenix in a book I was reading. My immediate thought was that these birds must be real, for how else could the bird I had dreamt about be in a book?

I still ask today, how can the same bird have been seen and depicted by so many cultures throughout the ages? Could they have actually existed? For some, they must be real, or at least have been real at one time. Could the memory of such a bird have been stored and passed down in our DNA?

There is still so much of our genetic code we have yet to understand. From what we've learned, we think we know that genes determine both physical and cognitive attributes such as pigment and possibly personality. We even speculate that genes do somehow contribute to memory. It's not too farfetched to also speculate that there may be a specific gene passed on to offspring, either from one or both parents, whose function is to carry on memories stored in the parent's or parents' DNA. Personally, I believe humans receive memories from both parents. This would explain why it's easier for some people to quickly learn multiple languages. It's said that it is easier for someone of Japanese descent to learn Japanese, even if that person is born in another country and has never heard the language spoken before, than it is for someone of European descent.

I grew up with Japanese, French, German, Hebrew, and English as the spoken languages in my household. I am genetically Japanese, Chinese, and Cherokee. I find it interesting that although I grew up with exposure to a plethora of languages, I still struggle with certain ones. I didn't know until I was twenty that my grandmother was half Chinese, and I wasn't exposed to the language. However, it turns out I was able to quickly learn just from hearing it here and there. I would say it's like deep down somewhere I already knew it.

If languages can be passed on and stored in our genetic memory, could we have within us "The Tower of Babel"? Imagine if we could unlock specific information, such as lost languages, from our own stored memories. There are so many ancient civilizations for which we've been seeking the secrets of their lost history. Questions we still, with all our modern technology, cannot answer. Within our subconscious memories, passed on to us from our ancestors, could there be forgotten information that no level of achievable technology may ever be able to uncover? The potential for technology is limited. The potential for evolution, however, is incalculable. It may just be that we are still too young for our current comprehensive capabilities to consciously access and apply the insight of past experiences. Therefore, are we designed instead to store those experiences in our subconscious where they are safely kept from our waking, functional perception? Over time as we live our lives and create new experiences of our own to add to the collective genetic memory, could some of the information stored make it into our awareness?

Is that how consciousness is formed? Do we build what we call "perception", "reality", and "consciousness" from a slow recollection of past, and possibly ancient, experiences? If so, then our waking perception is just a very small portion of "the world or the state of things as they actually exist". I wonder if our subconscious is the primary contributor to "reality", and if the definition of reality should instead be rewritten as 'the collected experiences, and interpretations of those experiences, gathered and continuously expanding indefinitely'. Or, to put it simply, is reality just in our heads?

Perhaps that's why we seem to instinctually accept concepts such as flying machines, ancient powerful weapons, visitors from the stars, floating cities and so on. When we see these concepts we once believed to be science fiction come to life, we don't react in awe or shock. Instead, it's as if we already somehow knew them to exist. When we explore the legends from various ancient cultures, we find references to these same concepts.

Some believe that mankind has simply been fantasizing about some of these technologies for that long and has since realized those fantasies only in the last few centuries. Others believe that some of the ritualistic practices of ancient cultures allowed certain people, often called prophets, to foresee these inventions. Ancient Astronaut and Ancient Time Traveler theorists believe that these technologies were witnessed during those times or possibly even before the first written history. We will visit both of those theories a bit later, and I will put forth my own explanation for how such technologies might've existed in the ancient past. However, for now I propose that they may have existed and are locked away within us. Are we tapping into the memories of previous technologies to reinvent them by accessing information stored in our DNA?

There have been many great minds throughout history who claim that their ideas and inventions came to them through visions, premonitions, or dreams, which suggest they were accessing the knowledge unconsciously. Some have been able to purposely reach other planes of consciousness through sound, relaxation, and meditation. There is a great deal of genetic material within us which scientists believe to be innate, unused junk. What if instead, that material is the physical manifestation of genetically stored memory? What if the majority of our DNA is merely a jumbled-up collection of matter containing the memories and information necessary to form consciousness?

If this is what it means to be aware, when did experience start? At what point did something happen to create the first memory? What was that something? If all reality is a collection of memories passed on through evolution, then that very first memory may be stored within us as well. Memories don't contain energy so they can't experience entropy, right? Or is there some kind of energy involved with creating and preserving memory? Are memories generating their own energy? Are they, themselves, energy? Is energy gained from experiences in order to convert those experiences into awareness? If so, can that energy, and potentially memories, be lost forever? If the very first memory was what some refer to as "The Big Bang", is it possible the occurrence created memory and energy as well as everything else? If over time the energy has deteriorated, is it also possible that the oldest stored memories, including the first, are beyond recovery? For now, I venture to think that the very first memory is still stored within us.

Is "reality" our perception formed by a collection of recollections, or are memories stored and passed down through genes? Perhaps the physical and metaphysical existences are not separate from one another. Whatever that first happening was potentially resulting in experience and memory, could it have created the physical and metaphysical universes simultaneously? Matter may simply be the canvas on which memory is painted. There may never be tangible evidence to support the theory of Genetic Memory, but awareness itself may stem from inherited memories.

A concept similar to this, which has some acceptance in the world of mainstream science, is Panpsychism. Panpsychism is the term describing the consideration that all matter contains some consciousness. If true, one could also suggest that consciousness can be transferred even to inanimate objects, which gives some credence to the existence of Mononoke. Could consciousness be imprinting on physical matter? Might this explain why some objects seem alive? Could it also explain why we seem to have an innate obsession with souls possessing or being trapped within certain items?

Many argue awareness is what makes us alive. To be alive is to be aware; to be conscious. Suppose, for example, there really was a "big bang". Now suppose that the big bang not only created all matter, and therefore the physical universe, but also a defining event which imprinted on that matter as the very first 'memory', thereby creating the metaphysical universe as well.

I'm not talking about the generally accepted "Big Bang" theory of how the universe was formed. That theory, in short, states that the universe was a small, dense, extremely hot 'singular' matter in which 'nothing' existed, not even time. The bang part is the sudden existence of time and/or perception as the universe, or the singular matter that was the universe, cooled and expanded. My problem with this is the idea that any matter existed prior to expansion and that it contained energy in the form of heat. Many still ask what happened before the "Big Bang" and what caused it. The truth is no one knows.

Therefore, what I am suggesting is that the actual "big bang" was in truth more of a small, slow forming of matter in a silent, singular event which simultaneously resulted in metaphysical existence as well. Quarks make up protons and neutrons which, with electrons, make up atoms and so on. There are six types of quarks, as far as we know, and quarks have charges. Many physicists don't consider quarks to be matter, but constituents of matter. If there was a singular mass that contained enough thermal energy to be the start of a very hot universe, what was it? It is suggested that prior to "The Big Bang" the universe was unspecified energy that came together to form matter and thermal energy. Could that initial matter have been electrons and quarks?

Instead of slow buildup of thermal energy, what if the initial defining event of all creation was caused by kinetic energy? How can kinetic energy exist without a force to act upon it? If vibration, or frequency, existed in the supposed hot dense pre-universe it could have built up kinetic energy at an immeasurably slow rate. Perhaps the natural frequency that existed prior to the universe's formation slowly vibrated quarks and other sub particles closer together generating heat. Then the combination of that thermal energy, kinetic energy, and frequency causing sub particles to vibrate and collide resulted in some sort of 'bang' like event in which the physical and metaphysical were created. If frequency can result in the creation of matter and potentially imprint some form of consciousness onto it, then perhaps in that universe creating moment the first memory was also imprinted on the resulting matter.

Instead, could a single defining event create an even smaller form of matter with a charge? That single event may have even been a thought or, as some have proposed, a dream. In any case, the initial morsels of matter came together as the universe cooled and expanded to create more which eventually led to quarks and leptons. Thus far, we believe that neutrinos are the lightest examples of mass and have no charge. Could the charge that particles and sub particles have be the energy I earlier referred to as potentially being memory? To put it another way, could sub particles be bits of tangible memory?

Regardless of how the physical universe was formed the question remains, could the metaphysical universe have been formed at that same moment resulting in memory, consciousness, perception, and awareness? If so, does it all continue to expand? Much like looking back to the earliest evidence of the physical universe, is there a way for us to tap into and look back at our earliest memories even if only on a subconscious level?

There's also the question as to whether consciousness and memory can exist without matter. Is matter merely the physical platform on which memory is inscribed to be passed along, or is it the tangible material that makes up consciousness, and therefore, awareness and memory as well? If memories do generate energy, might that energy be in the form of photons or a similar particle of light we've yet to discover? What role does light play in all this?

Light is made up of photons which have no mass, but carry and transfer energy, interact with matter, and can be absorbed by particles. Did photons come into existence during the initial event? Or might photons have been one of the colliding ingredients moved by the frequency of the universe? The human brain naturally produces biophotons. This means our brains generate energy in the form of light. Could the first interaction between a photon and matter have been the event that created everything including consciousness? Might light and/or consciousness be a living entity or entities?

Could physical beings who reach a higher understanding really ascend into the cosmos as light? Does this occur naturally to all living things upon death?

Did the energy of a photon, or photons, interact with matter in such a way as to initiate an eternal chain reaction resulting in the cycles of life, death, creation, destruction, and chaos? Can studying the tangible evidence our brains provide help us to understand consciousness? Just what is the exact correlation between what we call tangible and intangible? How does all of this relate to life, and specifically to life on Earth?

What is Life?

If you were to ask mainstream biologists what constitutes life, they would probably break it down into the eight characteristics of life we all learned in grade school. Those characteristics state that in order for something to be considered living it must; be made up of cells, be capable of reproducing, have genetic code, grow/change/develop, obtain and use materials for energy, respond to its environment, maintain homeostasis, and change/evolve over time. However, many believe that awareness is life. The question of what IS life has been a controversial source of debate for many people from different backgrounds going back centuries.

Assuming for a moment the definition provided by biologists is the accurate portrayal of living entities, under what category in that definition would awareness fall? I previously suggested that memory and consciousness could be written and stored into DNA, but awareness has been defined as an entirely separate concept. Biologists have also made claims that certain organisms, which they define as living, do not possess awareness. Would an entity need only to possess those eight characteristics to be considered 'alive' and does that render awareness irrelevant?

Some argue that awareness is what makes up a soul, but not life. However, there are those that believe all living things have a soul. Still, others believe that souls don't even exist. Where does consciousness, memory, and awareness fit into life? Where does the soul fit in?

When we determine an organism to be alive, we do so by verifying that it meets all the criteria of the eight characteristics. Cognitive function is studied separately. What about an entity that meets almost all the criteria and possibly has some form of consciousness? Viruses are not considered to be living entities because they do not possess cells and must commandeer genetic information from host cells in order to reproduce. However, they do possess RNA and, in some cases, even DNA which contains at least a portion of genetic code and while they may not contain cells of their own, they do inhabit and take over host cells to reproduce. There are several parasitic organisms considered to be living entities despite the fact that in order to live, use energy, and reproduce they must do so by infecting a host. Could viruses just be primordial parasitic forms that start out as non-living organisms and transition into living organisms once they've taken over a host cell?

Do viruses possess some awareness? If consciousness is a nonphysical characteristic of life, and what we consider to be consciousness are emotions, dreams, thoughts, memories and awareness, then would awareness and/or memories be enough to consider an entity as living? If awareness, at its most basic, is what enables an organism to respond to its environment shouldn't it be included as a defining characteristic of life? One of the stipulations is that an organism must be able to respond to its environment. Where does response come from?

Typically, if someone is considered non-responsive that individual is also considered unaware. Then does response stem from awareness on some level even if it's just instinctual? When something is considered instinctual it's thought to be a response written into genetic code. Therefore, shouldn't we think of awareness, as previously suggested, as written into genetic code as well?

What if the portion of genetic code that exists in RNA is the imprinted consciousness? RNA may have existed before and became DNA. If matter and consciousness were simultaneously formed and matter developed into RNA containing genetic memory and basic awareness, then can we classify viruses to be, at least basic, forms of life? Could we even consider them to be our original ancestors?

Does that mean all life originated from viruses? Could there have been other forms of RNA based entities that did not behave like viruses? Could they have instead obtained energy and reproduced by other means and without DNA or RNA? If so, did these entities eventually evolve and are they the creators of DNA? If DNA was created, and is therefore artificial, would this change how we define living organisms?

What's the point of all this? What reason might there be for matter containing awareness and memory and for RNA not only existing, but also having the ability to fold itself until becoming DNA? At what point did DNA obtain and store the other concepts of consciousness such as emotions, dreams, and thoughts? What do we include as life and what do we dismiss? Finally, what is the goal of life?

Meaning of Life

Another question that has been asked throughout the centuries and heavily debated by people of all backgrounds is the question of why life exists in the first place. There are those who believe it's all just one big coincidence and there is no meaning or design. Many people search for some sort of justification to our existence. This is probably due to a need for comfort either in knowing that there may be something better waiting for us after life, or in knowing that all we endure while in our physical forms serves a greater purpose.

To many, life can feel pointless, difficult, and even painful. It is so fragile and complicated in its design and, for humans at least, often brings with it physical and emotional suffering. It's almost as though humanity was never meant to be at all and is being punished simply for existing.

What if all that anguish does collectively have value? Whatever the connection between the physical and metaphysical worlds perhaps our suffering serves a significant purpose. If life is intended to endure torment and distress, could it be to make us welcome the end? Could death be the objective?

There has always been an understanding and a fascination with death throughout all life. We've even observed other species mourn when one of their own has died. We've seen unexpected behaviors in some that could be interpreted as spiritual and/or ritualistic. How many other organisms consciously acknowledge death?

If death is the goal of life, why do we mourn? Why are we filled with grief? In the various religions and belief systems, even of early humanity, we are taught that we should not fear death or be saddened by it. Instead, we are told to welcome it, to embrace it, for it is the end of suffering and the beginning of something else. Is it our loneliness and selfish feelings of abandonment that make us grieve? Are we merely feeling sad that it is not yet our turn to leave this existence? Is our grief and loneliness just a longing to follow our loved ones to whatever awaits after life?

Egyptologists believe that the Ancient Egyptians spent most of their lives preparing for death and that to them, it wasn't the physical existence that mattered, but the journey of the consciousness. The ancient people of Egypt appeared to believe a person's consciousness left the physical body upon death to travel to another realm.

Is life intended to prepare us for death? Are painful experiences inflicted upon the living imprinted on the consciousness and carried to another realm? Or is life nothing more than a concurrence mistakenly and coincidently created as a byproduct from the formation of matter and consciousness? If life is an error, is death the correction?

Death is considered an inevitability of life and has held profound meaning to many cultures. It has even been worshiped. There are so many ancient civilizations who believed death meant returning to the cosmos. If the universe came into being simultaneous to and possibly resulting from matter and consciousness, could this instinct within us to return to cosmos have been left by the original memory of creation? Is death merely matter and consciousness returning to the cosmos as a result of deterioration?

There are those who look to extend life and those who fear death. Is there within us a constant struggle between life wanting to continue and evolve and death attempting to correct and possibly prevent excess? There is at least one living organism that seems to have achieved at least some form of immortality. There is a jellyfish that continually recycles itself, so it's as though it never dies.

In actuality, the jellyfish does go through life stages and does succumb to a form of death under certain circumstances. Immortal isn't the same as invincible and they can still be killed, but if nothing interferes it could theoretically regenerate indefinitely. Is the number of times a single jellyfish can revive truly infinite? What id loses a little of itself each time? Might that limit how many reincarnations a single jellyfish can have? Could each life cycle also be shorter than the previous? Or is this already incredible ability done with enough efficiency to avoid attrition?

Although the new jellyfish which results from the old one recycling itself appears to be a perfect genetic clone, does it retain any awareness of all its experiences, or are the memories of its existence prior to trans differentiation lost in the process? If memories do contain energy in some form, could there be an exchange happening that allows the jellyfish to be reborn without any physical erosion by utilizing that energy? If memories are lost, where do they go?

If memory imprints on genetic material, then surely the new jellyfish would retain it somehow. After all, the current jellyfish is genetically identical to the previous. Does the jellyfish only lose the energy to consciously access the memories of its prior selves? Is obtained learning from experiences of past incarnations stored as instinct? Could that imply a correlation between the speculative energy pertaining to memories and instinct? Or since the new jellyfish has more or less shrunk back down to a juvenile again, could the memories be compressed like some sort of genetic zip file?

Jellyfish aside, if death is the goal of life, why does life seem so persistent? Life is always creating, changing, expanding, adapting, and evolving such that it's almost volatile. Is life extending itself and thus, its experiences with the purpose of enriching death? Do the memories we make have a profound impact on death? Is death merely a form of ascension in which our cognitive existence is heightened and our biological one no longer necessary? Does our consciousness truly leave the body to rejoin the ether? Does it combine with consciousness from others to form a sort of collective database of experiences and information?

It has been suggested that the cosmos is merely a cyclical balance of life and death. Although we assign importance and definition to both matter and cognition to explain physical existence and consciousness, does it all amount to an ever-shifting conversation of life and death? Is death merely the return of life from a physical plane to the greater realm? Could our universe have emerged out of the death of a previous one? Could the entire cosmos behave like the immortal jellyfish? Might there be some potential probability in further studies of the immortal jellyfish to make discoveries relevant to the origins of the universe and ourselves?

If life is to endure suffering in the physical world and death is being freed from that suffering to rejoin the cosmos, why do some fear death? Doesn't it make sense to want to prepare for the freeing of our minds from our body and to welcome death? Did ancient cultures embrace this idea? Should we fear immortality instead? Many people are afraid of the possibility of living forever. Is that instinctual? What if what we think of as immortality is only removing ourselves from a greater existence for a lesser one in which we are stuck in the physical plane? Would an infinite life in this plane be eternal physical and emotional torment? Our current understanding is that even if we do find a way to prolong the breakdown of our bodies or transfer our minds into artificial bodies, our cognition would eventually deteriorate. If death can be defined as the meaning of life, could there be a different kind of immortality waiting for us beyond status?

What is the purpose of having so many different types of life? Is life a chaotic chain reaction spiraling out of control resulting in mutations and unpredictable, unintended forms? Or is there a greater, possibly intended design? How did life come to be on Earth? Has this planet had deliberate impacts on life, and even potentially on death? There have been so many different forms of life just on this planet alone, more than we will ever discover, and so many have already met with death. What was their significance? How has it all affected Earth and Humanity?

Life on Earth

There are many theories on how life on Earth came to be covering the fields of religion, philosophy, science, and everything in between, but in my opinion none of them seem to give a complete story. We have been told that we are all one people created from the same origin, whether it be evolution or by a divine power, and that we have only been around for a short while. We've also been told that we have acquired understanding and intelligence beyond that of our ancestors. Finally, we believe we are the superior species on this planet. From my viewpoint, none of these assumptions are absolute nor do they provide a complete picture.

My opinion is that humans are ignorant, arrogant, and outright wrong about almost everything much of the time. Life has been on Earth for some time and in many forms. Are we at best a paragraph in a cosmic novel still being written? A novel from which we haven't read the full beginning, and whereby some chapters seem to be missing? Even some of the best theories are unable to account for countless mysteries on Earth alone, yet we endeavor to solve those beyond this planet.

We've asked ourselves many times "why Earth?" and "are there other planets with life?", specifically "human life" or something akin to it. Science can give us many reasons for why this planet is ideal for supporting carbon-based life such as the sizes and positions of our sun and moon being 'coincidentally' perfect to Earth and our magnetic field providing protection from radiation and meteor impact, but there's still something missing.

How did these conditions come about? If our planet started out as molten rock, where did the initial ingredients of life come from? Could these precise conditions only happen once? Are there no other conditions, perhaps nearly identical, in which life could form elsewhere? Has everything been a big scientific coincidence? Has it all been a divine miracle? Was it the result of intent by other sentient beings to create these 'perfect' conditions and if so, who are they and how did they come to be?

To even begin to offer explanations for any of these questions we need to broaden our thinking and truly explore this planet without preconceived notions. I said, 'this planet' because shouldn't we start looking for answers closer to home before we jump out into space? While I do not believe Earth is the only planet out there with life, I do suspect that venturing into space and even finding life on other planets will ultimately offer few, perhaps no, explanations and instead challenge us even more by revealing only more questions. If we want to understand life on Earth, which includes ourselves, don't we first need to understand Earth?

We still know more about space than we do our own oceans, which are teeming with wondrous forms of life that could potentially offer us information about our own genome. By studying the DNA of some of the more unique aquatic life we have made some fascinating discoveries. We truly know so little about the current creatures on this planet, but we think we know so much about our own nature and evolution. Why are we eager to explore the history of the universe when there

21

are still so many missing pieces to our history on this planet?

I could ramble on about various aquatic life, like Sea Cucumbers, Tardigrades, Cephalopods, and other unique species on this planet, but there is much to discuss about human life. What are humans? How did humans come to be? What's the relationship between our various hominid ancestors? Are Hominidae unique to this planet or do other types of Humanoids thrive elsewhere? How did ancient humans achieve some of the architectural wonders of Earth? What does it even mean to be human?

There are several theories offering expositions to these questions. By exploring each one and pointing out where it may be lacking, I hope to incite further curiosity and future speculation. After I've addressed, summarized, and offered some additional thoughts on each theory, I will propose an alternative theory of my own. Once all potential histories have been presented, remaining questions and possibilities can be explored in greater detail. Keep in mind it is not my intent to criticize or to "disprove" anything. All these theories have merit and any, or even all, of them may very well one day have enough supporting evidence to be accepted as "proof". With an open mind consider with me the various theories pertaining to we humans of Earth.

Section Two

Creationism

Creationists believe that Earth and humanity were formed with purpose by a higher being or higher beings. Therefore, Creationism encompasses the various religions of the world comprising of the belief that we came to be from the intelligent intent and omnipotence of God or gods. The creation stories of Shintoism, Hinduism, Zoroastrianism, the Judaic religions as well as Norse, Egyptian, Babylonian, Mayan, Hopi, and Greek mythologies all contend that human life on Earth is the product of divinity.

Creationism is not exclusive. Many scientists, philosophers, theory crafters, and other inquisitive minds have religious beliefs. Belief in a specific creation story is no more restrictive than belief in Scientific Theories. An open mind can accept many beliefs and in comparing all the explanations, religious and scientific, of how we may have come to be interesting connections become more apparent.

Just like with most Scientific theories, most creation stories describe there being a vast, black, and silent nothingness. Interestingly, the Shinto creation story describes this nothingness as silent chaos or shapeless matter. Then there was sound from the movement of particles. Is this movement describing vibration? Might this be referring to the natural frequency of the universe?

With the sound of moving particles came light which,

along with the most buoyant particles, rose and became Takamagahara from which came the first three gods. Two more followed shortly and these five gods are referred to as Kotoamatsukami with the original three being the creator gods, or Zokasanshin. Then the first two gods of the Kamiyonanyo were born followed by the five pairs. The last pair, Izanagi and Izanami, created the archipelago of Japan and gave birth to its many kami.

The Hindu religion also incorporates different generations of gods. However, unlike most religions, even other polytheistic ones, there are a few creation stories to consider. One such story is that of Vishnu awakening and pulling a lotus from his navel while floating on an ocean of milk on the serpent, Sesha. From that lotus appeared the god Brahma who went about creating everything. Another describes Brahma as having created the universe from himself.

In Hinduism everything, including creation, is cyclical. Brahma and Vishnu create and preserve, and the god Shiva destroys. If creation has happened several times, it makes sense that there would be multiple creation stories. Is there an eternal cycle of creation and destruction? Could the reason for their being multiple stories be due creations of more than one universe?

In Zoroastrianism the creator beings are described as opposing forces rather than gods. Ahura Mazda is the force of benevolence and light while Angra Mainyu is the force of malevolence and dark. They existed in separate locations independent of one another with Ahura Mazda being the creator and Angra Mainyu the destroyer. In Zoroastrianism humans have the freedom of choice and therefore our consequences are of our own doing.

The Babylonian creation story also has two creators,

Aspu the culmination of Earth's underground fresh waters and Tiamat the primordial seas. From the mixing of their waters came the birth of the Babylonian gods.

Like the other polytheistic creation stories up to now, the Norse, Egyptian, and Greek mythologies also describe family trees of gods. The founding god of Norse mythology was a giant from which the first gods grew out of various parts of his body as he slept. Ymir may have also been responsible for other creatures, as a six-headed beast came from his legs and he's considered the ancestor of all giants, which may or may not be human.

The Greek mythos also begins with a single being existing in black nothingness beginning the family tree of the gods. The black bird Nyx sat in the nothingness on a golden egg from which the first god, Eros the god of love, hatched. The top half of the egg became Uranus, and the bottom became Gaia representing sky and earth. From them came Kronos, from Kronos came Zeus, and from Zeus came Prometheus who created humans.

Common elements of ancient polytheist creation stories seem to be a black nothingness and/or primordial waters from which a founding deity or founding deities establish a lineage of gods, serpent-like entities being of significance and having affiliation to water, and humans being inconsequential. The Mayan creation story also places its founding gods in primordial waters. However, the creation of humans is somewhat unique in that it took the gods three tries using different material, the successful material being white and yellow maize. The Hopi legend is also a bit unusual with humans being made from dirt mixed with the saliva of a spider woman. Earth has been ladened with legends by countless cultures spanning an immeasurable progression of time. Did even our earliest ancestors concern themselves with why and how they came to be?

Although monotheistic religions do not have a family tree of gods, they do have levels of celestials and familiar lineages. To avoid a needlessly lengthy narrative of repetition, the Judaic bible creation story will be given with the creation stories of the other monotheistic religions to be described as how they differ. It should also be noted that while many consider Judaism to be the oldest monotheist religion, Zoroastrianism is sometimes considered to be the eldest due to Ahura Mazda being worshipped singularly as the creator. The earliest known references to there being a single divinity was from Plato and later Aristotle, both of whom influenced Judaism.

The Hebrew Bible tells two versions of the Genesis creation story and later references another. There have been many considerations for this from a variety of sources and interpretations are still being offered today. Suffice to say it is left to the individual to reconcile any presumed conflictions, which may be as it was intended. Again, in the interest of avoiding extraneous explanations the Biblical creation story will be told as one general summary with the differences of Genesis 1 and Genesis 2 highlighted as we come to them.

In the beginning God created the Heaven and Earth. He also creates plants, animals, man, and woman. The first difference between Genesis 1 and Genesis 2 is the description of time with Genesis 1 specifying six days and a seventh of rest and Genesis 2 accounting all creation as a continuous creation event potentially denoting only one day. The second difference is the order in which everything is created. Genesis 1 describes the creation of the ecosystem before the simultaneous creation of Adam and Eve. However, Genesis 2 describes creating Adam out of dust, sometimes written as clay, then putting him in a garden to work.

His presence moved through the waters and he said, "let there be light". Genesis 1 describes a formless, chaotic, dark, and watery deep while Genesis 2 describes streams coming up from the Earth watering the land. Although clearly worded differently, could these be describing the same waters? Water from deep, dark caves can also form streams on the surface.

God creates a paradise filled with plants and animals. In Genesis 1 he creates Adam and Eve together as the last in his series, while in genesis 2 only Adam is created and then everything else is seemingly done for him. Animals were made to help him work the garden and keep him from being lonely. With none of the animals being suitable helpers God puts Adam to sleep and creates Eve out of his body.

The Catholic, Mormon, Muslim, Jehovah, Baptist, Protestant, and other Christian religions have some variation of the Genesis creation stories. The Hebrew Bible contains additional information not found in most other variants.

The third potential reference to creation is found later in the Bible in which God is described as having slain Leviathan, a dragon in the sea that God divided, which has also been a subject of contention at times. Presumably, this refers to the Canaanite gods Baal and Yam, and in the Bible the Canaanites are depicted as evil, licentious idol worshipers who God orders killed.

Archeology and what little history we have of the Canaanites give us an entirely different portrayal, but they were a Mesopotamian civilization with gods comparable to the Babylonian gods Aspu and Tiamat. Baal is associated with storms which raise or even create rivers and rain is a source of fresh water which correlates to Aspu being Earth's fresh waters. Likewise, Tiamat and Yam are often termed as deep and/or raging seas. Could the Canaanite gods Baal and Yam be the Babylonian gods Aspu and Tiamat?

There are so many translations and interpretations of ancient writings and oral legends that refer to battles involving serpents, rivers, and seas. Could we be misunderstanding the concepts? What if serpents, which we tend to associate with snakes or dragons, are actually rivers and seas? Couldn't the translation of "twisting serpent" be a reference to a "winding river"? If a winding river branched off into seven more rivers and streams could the words of ancient Mesopotamians have been mistranslated into a "twisting serpent with seven heads"?

With languages constantly changing and there being so many, several drastically differing, how inaccurate might some ancient lingual analyses be? Some current mythoi contend that rivers are dragons or the spirit of dragons. In others, rivers have or represent spirits. Rivers provide fresh water relating them to life. Nearly all creation stories meaningfully involve water. If serpents are frequently included with great importance, are language barriers hindering modern conception?

Irrespective of their validity, the creation accounts all have comparable elements. Most describe a dark chaotic nothingness and primordial waters, the sudden creation of light and life from divinity, and humans being made from earthen materials such as dust, clay, or corn. Several imply humans were intended to serve.

Serpents frequently play essential roles and, while its common for them to be associated with water, wisdom, and freedom, it is less common for them to be malevolent. However, for some reason they were often "conquered" by a later deity.

Not only do creation myths share parallels with one another, but their descriptions of the event or events denoting the construct of the universe follow similarly to those of the recognized scientific theories. The ancient creations stories may all be describing the same thing, only differing in terms used from those of the scientific community. Much like a past community may have confused the language of another, could we all be making the same argument in different terms? Are we not understanding one another? Or are we all just not listening to each other? In further exploring the scientific terminologies renditions of creation, should we also consider the resemblances to some religious accounts?

The Theory of Evolution

There's a good chance that just about everyone has heard of Darwin's Theory of Evolution. It is probably one of the most accepted human origin theories and the one many of us are taught in school. Like many great thinkers of his time, Charles Darwin believed that the various forms of life came about through millennia of adaptation and natural selection resulting in evolution. His theory was that as an organism encountered potentially problematic challenges, be it environmental, predatory, or otherwise, that organism would have to react to those challenges and change in some way that would enable it to survive. Organisms unable to adapt and survive perished making way for new organisms. Darwin believed the extinction of those species explained why there are "missing links". Darwin's proposed mechanism for evolution is what's commonly recognized as "survival of the fittest".

In the one-hundred and fifty years since Darwin published his theory there have been numerous additions. While many scientists agree with Darwin's suggestion that life evolves, not everyone agree with his proposed catalyst of "survival of the fittest". Hence, various theories of how and why evolution occurs have offered alternative mechanisms. Some scientists borrowed or expanded upon ideas that existed before Darwinism.

Some of the earliest thoughts about how there came

to be variations in organisms come from Plato and Aristotle. Though not actual evolution theories, they do attempt to explain life through observing and hypothesizing about nature instead of conceding everything to creationist ideology. Aristotle believed that the world and higher life forms, such as humans, had existed since eternity. Aristotle's theory of a fixed hierarchy was later expanded on to include the creationist concept of God by suggesting the ladder of life was created by God as an intended chain.

Plato believed in Organism and the metaphysical universe. Organism postulates that the universe and everything in it is alive and ordered. As for Plato's specific take on life, he considered life in the terms of form, appearance, and physical. The form he considered to be an idea or concept and therefore unchangeable, like an object's basic foundation or definition. The appearance of a form depends on shadow and perception. Anything physical can be changed and forms can have different representations. Plato's philosophies neither suggest nor contradict evolution. If the universe is alive and physical entities are subject to change and variations in appearance evolution could just be a part of it.

Some other earlier evolution theories before and during Darwin's time were Lamarckism, Orthogenesis, Vitalism, Structuralism, Catastrophism, and Mutationism. Each proposes alternative reasons for changes in organisms. Lamarckism is the theory of evolution that proposes organisms can acquire traits which they then pass on to future generations and through gradual generational changes those traits are passed on through genes. Orthogenesis is the theory that life has an instinctive internal objective to evolve into higher forms of life and contends that all organisms process a driving force within them to direct them towards change. Vitalism suggests change occurs because of the soul. Structuralism argues that the bodies of life forms are shaped due to a natural plan. Catastrophism suggests that the planet, and/or parts of the planet, endured extinction events due to natural disasters which lead to the organisms wiped out during the events being replaced by new life forms. Mutationism is the sudden changes from previous species into new ones. Modern Synthesis combines various aspects of the early evolution theories and considers multiple mechanisms. Evolution could be occurring through any combination of the proposed mechanisms and for a variety of catalysts.

Could another potential catalyst for evolution be the introduction of DNA altering compounds through consumption of unintended food sources? Perhaps as environments changed or organisms migrated they ingested substances or other organisms their bodies weren't designed to. We know ingesting certain compounds can have profound, even permanent, effects on brain chemistry. Could changes in diet have caused metabolic adaptations and/or mutations resulting in evolution?

Organisms develop mutations for a variety of reasons. One such reason is due to environmental factors which force a genetic change. A helpful genetic change is considered an adaptation. As that genetic adaptation is passed on to future generations to ensure their survival it may cause other changes within the species or result in an entirely new species. Genetic changes from one species to one or more new species is evolution. Without adequately preserved fossils of every species that ever existed on our planet it can be challenging to determine evolutionary relationships between today's thriving populations.

We can map genomes and compare the genetic information of various species to determine relationships between them and ourselves. Sharing genetic information with other species can add support to The Theory of Evolution but does not offer absolution.

Another explanation for shared genetic information may be due to the limited ingredients on this planet. Could it be that the elements and genetic information available on Earth severely differ from elsewhere in the galaxy? What if similar combinations of life developed, adapted, and evolved separate from one another using the same ingredients? For example, if five different chefs were given the exact same ingredients and asked to make a meal with them, wouldn't they likely each come up with a different recipe? The result would be different meals comprised of the exact base ingredients.

As for human evolution, there are several additional theories concerning the origins of modern humans. The Out of Africa Theory argues that Homo Sapiens developed in Africa and then spread throughout the world. The less accepted Multiregional Theory suggests that earlier ancestors, such as Homo Erectus, evolved in Africa and migrated to other regions before eventually giving way to modern Homo Sapiens likely by interbreeding with Homo Sapiens.

It is suspected that Homo Sapiens became the dominant species either by conquering all other early hominids or by interbreeding with them until only Homo Sapiens remained. Could this be how Neanderthals disappeared? The Out of Africa Theory contends that Homo Sapiens conquered other hominids before migrating out of Africa, while the Multiregional Theory believes other previous human ancestors migrated to other regions of the planet before merging with Homo Sapiens through interbreeding. Both theories can be considered sub-theories of Evolution and contend that humanity's origins stem from Africa.

It would seem that no matter which theory of human evolution is proposed, the common element is that human ancestors came from Africa. Why? Is Africa the incubator of Earth? What makes Africa the only possible place from which any hominid species to have evolved? Is this assumption due to the discovery of Mitochondrial Eve? While she may have been one of the earliest Homo Sapien mothers, but she is still Homo Sapien and therefore occurred after many of our earlier ancestors and cannot account for their lineages. So why do we insist all other species, like Neanderthal and Denisovans, evolved from Africa as well?

The Ancient Astronaut Theory

The Ancient Astronaut Theory is one that has gotten a lot of attention in recent years but has been around for some time. This is the theory that suggests that the ancient ancestor, or ancestors, to humanity came from somewhere other than Earth. There are many sub-theories to explain how this could've happened and this theory also overlaps with others that we'll explore later. For now, if we consider the possibility for a moment, could our ancestry be extra-terrestrial?

Most often it is suggested that we are either the off-spring of an advanced forgotten race that came to Earth for any number of reasons thousands of years ago, or the result of those visitors genetically manipulating the indigenous ancestors already here. The theory states that we were visited, possibly are still being visited, and that visitation or visitations somehow resulted in humans as defined today.

Another variation of this is the theory of Directed Panspermia in which Earth was seeded by the DNA of extraterrestrials and evolved into the various life forms that now exist. An extension of this theory is that the seeding is still happening today through additions of genetic material being intentionally introduced at specific stages by means of comet and/or asteroid delivery in order to continue the manipulation of life on Earth.

There is also the consideration that an accidental Panspermia may have taken place. It is suggested that life was seeded here by means of genetic information falling to Earth from space, but not necessarily by design. We know it's possible for some microbes to survive the harsh conditions of space. Perhaps some genetic information from another planet made it to Earth entirely by accident.

Assuming the whole thing was somehow a big extraterrestrial accident and Earth was seeded by genetic information falling to earth from debris, does that mean humanity is another significant coincidental byproduct? Just look at the specific conditions that had to be exactly right at exactly the right time for humans on Earth to have been an incalculable accident. The first condition had to be the exact placement of Earth in what's referred to as the Goldilocks zone. Earth had to be positioned not too close and not too far from the sun in order to be just the right temperature. The second and third conditions are Earth's moon being exactly the right size as well as exactly in the right position relative to Earth. The fourth condition is Earth's protective magnetic field and atmosphere. The Fifth condition being that genetic material had to survive space and fall to this planet.

I could further dissect each of the aforementioned conditions, but I think we can extrapolate that for our existence to have been a cosmic accident, though very possible, is a difficult explanation for many to accept. It certainly would be easy enough to dismiss it all as chaotic cosmic coincidence and look no further, but many are unable and unwilling to believe this is the ultimate answer to both how and why we are here. Homo Sapien DNA is so complex that many scientists argue the odds of it having been created naturally are astronomical.

If we instead consider that we were intentionally

seeded by Panspermia, then it starts to make sense that all the conditions were just right. There are many who believe those conditions were engineered ahead of seeding the planet to ensure success. If there exist advanced enough beings out there capable of intentionally seeding a planet, is it certainly possible that those beings created the perfect planet on which to do so? One theory is that Earth may be an experiment. Others believe that it wasn't done out of curiosity, but out of necessity. It is possible that instead of Earth serving as a place of scientific research and development, it is a new beginning intended for the survival of life.

The Fermi Paradox contends that with such a high probability for life elsewhere in the universe there should be regular interplanetary activity, but instead there appears to be very little evidence of extraterrestrial interaction. Thus, the Zoo hypothesis proposes that humanity is not yet ready for such interactions and evolution on Earth is merely being observed from afar to avoid interfering with the natural process. This could mean our planet is an artificially created environment in which natural evolution is being studied. It could also mean when higher beings happened upon this planet, they determined it to be in an early stage of development relative to their own and saw it as an opportunity to learn how life evolves.

As for the genetic manipulation of life on Earth, it has been suggested that human evolution has been specifically guided. Some argue that human beings are unlike any other forms of life on this planet due to peculiar leaps in our genetic evolution that scientists can't account for or properly justify. Some ancient astronaut theorists believe not only that extraterrestrials have visited Earth and altered our DNA in the past, but that they are doing so even today. They propose that the reason could have been to artificially evolve a life form that already existed here on Earth to over time become more genetically compatible with their genome.

Other ancient astronaut theorists point to various religious and cultural creation stories about "gods" interbreeding with humans and interpret those stories as historical accounts of extra-terrestrial hominids interbreeding with early human ancestors which resulted in modern humans. It is thought that perhaps a human-like species of extra-terrestrial beings came here as explorers or to mine Earth's minerals and became interested in the various species that already existed here. There's speculation that they may have even intentionally interbred in order to create hybrids.

Could it be that Homo Sapien Sapien is not an indigenous species to Earth? Could Homo Sapiens be an invasive species? Might this explain why Homo Sapiens replaced all other hominids? If so, how might that have changed evolution on this planet and what might the potential consequences be? If Homo Sapiens are an invasive species and were created or brought to Earth by design was it done by a highly evolved race of beings from another planet?

Now any, or even all, of these events could have taken place resulting in new evolutionary mutations eventually culminating into what we think of as humans today. Ancient Astronaut theorists also claim that some of the architectural wonders of ancient times can also be explained by extra-terrestrial influence.

One problem with many of our various current beliefs is that they have been unable to explain with any satisfaction how ancient humans, who were supposed to have been significantly inferior by today's standards, were able to achieve technological and architectural feats that we cannot even replicate with today's technology. The Ancient Astronaut theory is one widely accepted belief that does provide an explanation.

There are also some discrepancies in the archeological and geological timeline. Monuments and civilizations that were believed to have been built no more than a few thousand years ago are being reexamined today due to new evidence that they are much older. However, if these monuments and ancient cities really are many thousands of years older, could human ancestors really have been the ones to build them? If they were built by ancient humans, when and how was this achieved? The Ancient Astronaut theory proposes that ancient humans had help, or at least knowledge that has since been lost, from extra-terrestrial visitors.

Does this theory alone give us a complete picture of human evolution? I find the ancient astronaut theory to be intriguing as well as plausible, but it still leaves a few holes. Also, there are other theories that provide the same level of explanation while being just as intriguing and equally plausible.

Ancient Time Travelers

As modern humans with all our technological advances and our science fiction entertainment, we like to think of ourselves as being on the cusp of achieving dominance over all arts, sciences, philosophies, and disciplines. We even believe ourselves capable of one day having complete control over space and time, thereby being able to manipulate and travel through both at will. Therefore, one theory that has been put forward is that it has already been done.... well not yet.... but will be and thus has been.

The theory of Ancient Time Travelers suggests that in the future we will have created a means by which to travel through time and space and by traveling back in time to our ancient past we will enable our future. To simplify, instead of our ancient ancestors having been visited by extraterrestrials from some other planet, they may have been visited by our future descendants from Earth like a sort of self-fulfilling prophecy. This would fit perfectly with the views of both Plato and Aristotle as an eternal cycle of human existence. Perhaps those time travelers even got stuck in the ancient past and were unable to return to their correct timeline. They then shared their knowledge and lived their lives and interbred with ancient hominids of the past.

Many don't care for alternate timeline or alternate reality theories in general, often due to their paradoxical nature, but we cannot dismiss them either. It is my personal belief that "time", as in progression, only travels forward and we can only move forward through it. I believe we can accelerate time around us without aging ourselves and therefore travel into the future, but that the past has already happened and even though we may be able to view the past I am hesitant to believe we can move backwards to it. This obviously does not include time zone situations such as traveling from Japan to the U.S. and arriving at your destination yesterday.

What I mean to say is that time is a human concept and while we would like to believe that we could revisit and possibly even alter what has already happened it is my personal belief that the closest we can come is to somehow view the past and witness certain events. For example, if a human being was caught in an energy field which allowed the viewing of all of time and space simultaneously, he or she might be able to witness the past, present, and future. Supposedly this has happened to some individuals in the past, like Nikola Tesla getting caught in an electrical field during one of his experiments. I wouldn't recommend trying this.

It is suspected that certain energy phenomenon may cause vortexes which connect various points in time and/or space. They may also connect our plane of existence with another. If the frequency at which matter vibrates determines the plane or dimension in which that matter exists, then theoretically an energy field or vortex capable of altering that frequency could transport matter into alternate times, space, and/or realities. Is the change in frequency of that matter then permanent? What happens to that matter if it returns to its original natural vibration after the vortex dissolves? Would it reemerge back into the time, space, or dimension from which it originated? Or would it become trapped? If matter became trapped in an alternative dimension for which its natural frequency is incompatible, would that matter dissolve, implode, explode, or experience cascading failure?

However, it is currently supposed and accepted by many scientists that we can potentially travel through time in both directions. This is why, for some, the Ancient Time Traveler theory is more acceptable than humanity evolving from ancient alien ancestry. I certainly am no expert and therefore can only offer alternative theories to the contrary. As such, could time travel also offer explanations for the various mysteries of our past? Perhaps it shouldn't be ruled out.

It is suggested that tools and even weapons from the future may have been used in the ancient past to both create and destroy. This would explain how such structural enigmas were so precisely created and why we see evidence in more than one ancient site of nuclear war. It might also explain ancient depictions of machines that were not invented until centuries later and why some ancient texts describe aerial battles.

Just like with the Ancient Astronaut theory the Ancient Time Traveler theory, while providing intriguing arguments, does not provide a complete picture. With both theories there seem to be missing pieces, like missing chapters to a story.

The Holographic Universe Theory

For those who prefer the more mathematical approaches to existential theories, the Holographic Earth Theory provides an alternative view of ourselves and the planet. Physicists are considering the theory that somewhere out in distant space there is enough information to project a two-dimensional world in the same way as a hologram is projected.

This is still an actively debated theory primarily among Physicists and mathematicians due to certain conundrums becoming less problematic when the universe is viewed in two dimensions rather than three. For example, there are a lot of questions concerning the nature of black holes and gravity which seem to make more sense in two dimensional models as opposed to three dimensional ones.

What does that mean for us? Are we also holograms? Are we living inside a hologram? Do our physical bodies exist somewhere else while our minds are being projected into a digital world? Do we even have physical bodies? Are we just a series of computer code? Perhaps we really are made up of light being projected onto a two-dimensional plane. Could this explain some of the more bizarre happenings in our world like the Bermuda Triangle and cases of whole villages vanishing? Are these just computer glitches?

Computer code making up all that exists does work from a mathematical perspective, but keep in mind our understanding of math may be limited. When we consider the understanding, we've gained in the last half century, it's entirely possible that we've barely scratched the surface. To me it seems like we're only working with a portion of the graph and disregarding numeric values which fall into portions we don't understand. If some advanced entity does exist elsewhere, our accumulated mathematical knowledge may be laughable in comparison.

It's also possible that we are comprised of binary code in a digital existence created solely for the purpose of entertaining higher beings. We may be the product of projecting a hypothetical world for others to view. Who are these others and why would they want to view this world? The speculation is still underway, and there are possibilities abound.

Focusing specifically on the current Holographic Universe Theory, it does seem to have some usable insight. However, like most theories, it also comes with flaws. The Holographic Universe theory can help us solve some difficult equations, but only by making assumptions that we are far from having enough data to make. There is also the matter of perception and tangible observations which seem to contradict this theory and, conversely, are called into question by it.

The theory also incorporates concepts from String Theory and from particular points of Einstein's General Relativity. The issues arise when we try to apply these concepts to a three-dimensional universe containing matter. You could argue that in a two-dimensional projection the tangible concept of matter doesn't exist. If everything is merely a holographic projection, did only the metaphysical universe come into being? Was the first event from which existence was created the first thought? Was it sudden awareness? Does everything only exist as consciousness? Is everything, including

46

humans, a cosmic dream created by swirling energy? Does an older awareness exist somewhere manipulating ours into a hologram or possibly even a dream?

The Lovecraft Universe

If we're going to go down a rabbit hole of reality being not but a dream, we may as well consider the universe described by H. P. Lovecraft in his Cthulhu Mythos. The Cthulhu Mythos is the name given to Lovecraft's combined settings and deities from his series of horror novels.

This fictional collection describes an existence created from the dream of a god called Azathoth without Azathoth having any knowledge, and therefore likely no intent, of its creation. It is said that when Azathoth awakens, existence ends.

There is a plethora of other gods, but their existence also seems to be a part of Azathoth's dream. I say seems to be because this is still a much-debated point among fans of Lovecraft's work and there are many interpretations. In his work Azathoth is said to dream all reality, which I personally interpret to include the other gods even if they exist outside of the universe.

If all reality is a dream, that does not mean that a god or entity of any kind must have dreamt it. Assuming all existence is a dream and dreams are made up of thoughts, awareness, and subconsciousness swirling through energy in the cosmos, there only needs to be radiation. There is plenty of radiation in space.

Is our entire existence merely a dream caused by the decay of particles in space? Could there be an entity dreaming all of reality? Could there actually be several sub-atomic particles giving off enough energy to cause consciousness, subconsciousness, awareness, and consequently a massive dream known to us as reality? Or do we exist in a tangible form made up of matter on a physical sphere held together by gravity?

The Artificial Earth Theory

The Artificial Earth Theory brings us back to the physical world suggesting that not only is Earth tangible, but also artificially created. This theory could easily tie into The Ancient Astronaut, The Ancient Time Traveler theories or even the Hollow Earth Theory which suggests that Earth is hollow, or the interior has a significant void. If the Earth was artificially created, was it done by Aliens? Was it done by time traveling humans? Could it have been done by an ancient, advanced civilization on Earth? Is there another possibility?

Well, the Bible does say that God created this world and did so in only a few days. If God did create Earth, who or what is God? Could God be an Extra-terrestrial? Could God be a time traveler? Could God be a free-floating sentience who thought or dreamt Earth into being?

Putting the "who done it" aside for the moment, is it even possible to artificially create a planet? Is "artificial" even the right adjective for an omnipotent metaphysical being creating a planet out of the raw materials and forces of the universe, either knowingly or unknowingly?

If a planet can in some way be manufactured, for what purpose? Did other worldly beings orchestrate our entire existence by creating Earth? Was our entire solar system created by these same beings?

Part of the reason for the Artificial Earth Theory is that many believe the moon to be a purposeful artificial creation. The moon is perfectly sized and perfectly positioned. Some say it may also be hollow. If the moon was artificially created why not the Earth too? Likewise, if the moon is hollow, couldn't Earth be hollow as well? How much of the universe is artificial? Why not our whole solar system? How many universes are completely artificial?

Could Earth be special in that it's the only intentionally created planet? Why would someone or something intentionally establish a planet? Was Earth fashioned so its creator or creators could also form life or a specific life form like humans? Could the being or beings who created Earth have carved elaborate underground environments deep within its layers? If so, why? Did they make cities or research bases from which to monitor their creations? Or could there be thriving ecosystems preserving certain forms of life safely below Earth's surface? Could the origin of life on this planet actually come from someplace deep within the Earth, rather than from the surface? If Earth was specifically created in order to also generate and sustain life, are we the only life in the universe?

Did life emerge from deep, warm, safe places? Is that where we get the idea of a cosmic egg? Could life supporting planets be hollow and warm inside incubating life like eggs nesting in the cosmos? Did climate changes, curiosity, and/or other factors cause life forms to slowly migrate towards the surface? Or might some life forms have been suddenly uprooted by a drastic natural event such as an earthquake forcing them to adapt? Are such planets created through natural processes of the universe or are they artificial creations of higher sentience? If these planets, and potentially even the entire cosmos, are artificially creations of consciousness, could everything really be a holographic projection of that consciousness? Or could an ancient, but tangible source of life have evolved and created new life throughout the cosmos in the form of egg-like planets including Earth? If so, why?

Could Earth have been designed by advanced entities from planets that could no longer sustain life in an effort to preserve entire ecosystems from their worlds? Is Earth essentially the Noah's Ark of the universe? If Earth does sustain environments deep within its interior could exploration, such as that described in the Jules Verne novel Journey to the Center of the Earth, be possible?

The Agar Plate Theory

Why do we say, "the origin of life"? Why does life need a single origin? For that matter, why does life need any origin? If everything is cyclical and there's no end, there is also no beginning. If there are infinite possibilities, might there also be infinite origins? If there is only one origin, doesn't it seem likely that origin exists out in the cosmos and not on Earth? If the origin of life stems from the cosmos, why would it have only taken root on this planet? If life spread out throughout the cosmos and there are many planets with human-like beings on them, why should all humans on this planet come from a single source out of one location?

Did all life on Earth really come from a single source? Do living organisms really adapt to changes and eventually evolve as we've been taught? If so, is it from this process and from the occasional mutation that new organisms do arise? I'm sure this is at least part of the story. However, just like it seems rather narrow minded and outright silly to me that we would be the only planet in all the cosmos with life, it also seems wholly unrealistic that every living creature on this planet evolved from one single-celled organism.

I have a theory of my own to propose which I am hereby calling the Agar Plate Theory as that is the analogy I use when attempting to explain my hypothesis to others. This could be considered another theory of evolution, but also includes elements of the Ancient Astronaut and The Hollow Earth theories. My belief is that life did not originate from one organism on this planet and life occurring on Earth was not a singular event.

While I do believe life evolves and has been doing so for millennia, I do not think all the life on this planet came from one organism, or even one type of organism. I also don't think life occurred in one event or at one time. If the planet was a molten mess of elements that slowly cooled over time, it makes sense that the cooling would have occurred at different rates across the planet. It could be that the various molecule materials available at the time were just a mess of the basic elements, amino acids, and nucleotides which eventually formed into RNA and DNA. Or as asteroids and comets contributed to the materials of molten Earth they could have brought along strands of RNA and/or DNA. Viruses, bacteria and proteins could have also been falling to Earth. Regardless of how the ingredients got here, Earth was a teaming soup of molecular possibilities.

As that soup cooled molecular life changed and evolved. Assuming some locations of the globe cooled faster than others, the impact on microbial life could have varying effects on evolution at each location. Some areas of the planet may have seen the evolution of life slowed to a near standstill if the rate of cellular division drastically decreased due to potentially sudden and severe drops in temperature. While locations that remained hot saw an increase in microbial division, adaptation, and evolution. There may have also been discrepancies in the molecular material available per location.

The reason I compare this to an agar plate is because if you've ever seen colonies growing on an agar plate then you know they often grow independently of one another and at different rates. Assuming the Earth was like a giant prepared agar of amino acids and the incoming molecular materials were like a smear, evolution may have formed independently at different rates in colonies around the globe. Thus, we would have organisms all over the planet that started off the same or similar from the available ingredients, but due to their locations some developed into new organisms before others. Also due to their locations, environmental changes would likely have determined specific variants in new generations of organisms. Since the environments of hotter areas of the planet would have differed from those of cooler areas the adaptations made by the planet's organisms would have also differed according to their metabolic needs.

After a few millennia of adaptation and evolution, as well as the potential continuation of additional genetic material falling to Earth, the new generations of microbial life in each environment would have been very different from one another. The microbial life at colder locations may have experienced little to no change, while microbes in hotter locations may have already evolved into cyanobacteria and begun the next planetary change, which would have been the oxygenation of Earth. The atmospheric changes would have encouraged further evolution and again at different rates depending on the atmospheric effect on organisms in each location. It is also possible that cyanobacteria arrived on a meteor or comet prior to the cooling and had already begun altering the atmosphere thus initiating the terraformation of the planet sooner.

If life grew and evolved in separate colonies around the globe experiencing different factors of change along the way, then the colonies could potentially be in different stages of evolution and have had different adaptations according to locational attributes. From this we can suspect that later, more complex life forms from each colony would appear at various locations and times across the planet, some likely in nearly identical environments, but having completely different structures and appearances. However, due to having evolved on the same planet, these life forms could potentially be genetically close enough to produce offspring with one another eventually filling the planet with hybrids and leading to a multitude of new species.

What I'm saying is perhaps human life did not come from a single source. What if different types of hominids developed out of independent colonies of evolution and at different times on the planet from various locations? Could one bipedal creature evolve at one location on the globe at the same time as another? Could there have been different hominids popping up all over the planet, not from a single common ancestor, but from separate colonies of evolution? If there were some colonies that evolved in locations with similar climates or in locations that eventually mimicked previous climates of locations that cooled earlier, could there have been parallel evolutions of different colonies? Could some colonies even have produced more than one branch of Hominidae, but at separate stages of evolution, perhaps even thousands of years apart? Might these evolutions have been similar enough to produce bipedal creatures capable of interbreeding? Were some species more evolved than others? If some ancient hominids emerged thousands, potentially millions, of years before others, might they have still interacted with newer species and potentially have even been able to interbreed and produce viable offspring with them?

Another explanation for shared genetic information may simply be due to "limited ingredients". The elements and genetic information available on this planet may severely differ from those on another. Could it be that similar combinations of life developed, adapted, and evolved separate from one another, but with the same basic building blocks available? Isn't this part of why scientists believe other humans may exist on planets similar enough to Earth?

This possibility is why I say there are elements of the Ancient Astronaut Theory, Hollow Earth, and various Evolution theories. Even if life on this planet came about due to panspermia as many Ancient Astronaut Theorists propose, directed or otherwise, it still may have evolved from several different genetic trees at different rates. At least one tree might have even developed underground and emerged from caves as described by some cultures. The complex life we see at the poles now, such as ice worms, may be similar to evolved forms of life that existed millions of years ago in other locations. Furthermore, with new genetic information falling to earth every year, new evolutionary trees may be forming right under our noses that will later evolve into more dynamic beings like us millions of years from now. Could the process of single-celled life forms developing into new multi-cellular life which then further splits into diverse branches of complex life forms still be occurring? Has it been doing so in a cyclical nature for eons? Could we draw comparisons between this potentially perpetual cycle and the concepts of Plato, Aristotle, and Hindu eternal cycles of existence?

If true, there may have existed many variants of hominids at one point which could have evolved separately from different types of ancestral organisms at different locations and as they spread out and encountered one another slowly merged from several species of human into homo sapiens. This is where my perspective differs from both the out of Africa and the

Multiregional theories. Both say that humans evolved in Africa from a common ancestor and their only difference is whether we evolved into homo sapiens and then spread out, or if different ancestors of homo sapiens left at different times to be replaced by Homo Sapiens. The problem I have with both is that they have all of humanity evolving from one source and from one location. Both explanations assume that even other known ancestral hominids, such as Denisovans and Homo Floresiensis, which appear to pop up in complete isolation, somehow still originated in Africa and then traveled to their locations. What is so significant about Africa that all hominids must've come from this single location? Is Africa the womb of the planet?

What if one ancestor evolved in northern Asia, another the Icelandic region, another in Africa, another in Australia, another in South America and so on? Might each hominid's evolutionary line have originated from drastically different microorganisms like tardigrades, nematodes, and rotifers? Could we be looking at an early stage of hominin development every time we examine tardigrades? What if one of the ancient hominids found on Earth did evolve on another planet before coming here? If different types of hominids developed all over and eventually encountered one another, interbred, and then encountered new hominids and interbred with them, homo sapiens may be the result of a series of hybridization events.

What if Earth at one time was home to several different types of hominids from several different sources before bottlenecking to one? What sort of beings might have existed before us? Is this the reason for why there are stories of different beings in ancient myths? Could the different bipedal creatures have been more intelligent than previously believed? Could there have also been other sources of hominids besides parallel colonies of evolution of Earth? What if Homo Sapien is an invasive species introduced to our planet after the evolution of native inhabitants? Could Homo Sapien DNA have been too potent for the original Hominidae of Earth? Could this explain why a potentially large number of diverse hominid species dwindled down into one? If the recessive genetic information of previous hominids remains dormant with us today can this account for some rare genetic anomalies?

Before the early inhabitants succumbed to Homo Sapiens could Earth have been a "Tolkien-like" world? If so, might it have included races like vampires, elves, gnomes, angels, demons, giants, dwarfs, yetis and so on? Did the existence of these races inspire the various creation stories and mythos of the ancient world? Can we find evidence of their past civilizations? Could the one hundred and seventy-five stone skulls on the walls of Tiwanaku represent as many different intelligent bipedal species living on the planet simultaneously? Did the Andean people know and try to preserve a history of many races? Might the various statues, tikis, carvings, and paintings of unusual looking beings we find all over the world represent the diverse ancient cultures of a forgotten past?

Many different cultures have legends of a small race of people who were apparently gifted builders and metallurgists, giants who were stone masons capable of levitating monoliths, and amphibious or reptilian ancestral teachers who provided math, astronomy, and fire. If such a large number of ancient cultures describe the same types of ancestors, could they be describing some of the other unknown types of human ancestors that coexisted with the ones we're familiar with before the Homo Sapien bottleneck? Could some of these beings have had significantly longer life spans as also described by many ancient historical records?

If there were many fantastical prehistoric races and remnants of their genetic code slumbers within our own, could this be the cause of certain hereditary ailments? There are a couple of genetic disorders which scientists speculate may have been responsible for stories of vampires. Could a vampiric race have existed? If so, could the aforementioned disorders be a result of their latent DNA rather than a mutation? Might mutations have occurred not only due to interbreeding, but also consumption?

One proposed mechanism for evolution is consumption. It is thought that one single-celled organism engulfed another and became multicellular. It is also noted that some single-celled organisms incorporate certain material they encounter, like algae, into their own makeup. If ingesting certain plants containing brain altering chemicals has the potential to stimulate the brain in a beneficial way that's passed down to offspring, what might be the consequences of consuming the DNA of other species? Another shared legend among ancient cultures is that "the gods" would drink blood, eat specific body parts of conquered enemies, create special food or potions, and consume and utilize mana. Modern scientists study the possibility of cannibalism among certain human ancestors as well as the likelihood of different hominids killing and eating one another. If some of the various ancient races were consuming others, might this have also contributed to their evolution and the eventual extinction of those who were fed upon? Could this also be the foundation for legends of vampires and other beings who feed on human blood and/or flesh?

How many other "mythological" races might actually

have been ancient inhabitants of Earth? How much of our history have we dismissed as fanciful tall tales due to our own misconceptions? So many different ancient societies described dragons or winged serpents and often they are said to live in caves or underground. Could ancient people have really encountered such an organism when exploring cavern systems? Did this type of organism develop underground and is therefore unable to survive on the surface? Could there also be other bipedal creatures living safely in underground ecosystems? If so, might they have reptilian, or amphibious features and attributes? The origin stories of several North and South American native cultures describe their civilizations emerging from caverns and cave systems. Shouldn't we consider those stories plausible and likely true?

Also, if there were several races and cultures evolving all over the planet at different times, might that explain why so many legends of flying machines and sky gods exist? It's possible that some of the ancient hominids did develop flying and encountered other developing cultures as they explored the globe. Why do modern scientists dismiss the ancient stories of flying machines and visitors from the sky? Is it because they assume it must mean The Ancient Astronaut Theory is the only explanation? What if it was never beings from other planets? What if it was simply forgotten or unknown Earthlings all along?

If several different lineages did evolve all over the planet, some potentially separated by thousands or even millions of years, might a few of them have reached a level of civilization similar to or even surpassing ours today? By assuming humanity came from a single source and no greater beings or civilizations existed prior, what clues have we missed to other possible truths? Could some of those ancient races have been the ones responsible for the wondrously mysterious megalithic ruins all across the planet?

Section Three

The Cycle of History

One explanation as to why there would appear to be evidence of advanced civilizations prior to when we are told civilization began is, as mentioned before, the Ancient Astronaut Theory. If at one time extra-terrestrials did come to Earth and live among the various ancient humans as their "gods" they would've likely been advance enough to create massive monolithic cities. As for what happened to those beings and why the knowledge was lost, we can only be speculate.

Another reasonable explanation is, as also before mentioned, the Ancient Time Traveler Theory. If we do become capable of time travel in the future, we would likely also be capable of creating marvelous stone cities. Why would we travel into our ancient past to do so? Did time travelers build outposts for themselves to observe their ancient past? Were they unable to return to their own time and build cities for themselves in the hope of living separate from the rightful people of that time period so as not to interfere to much with the timeline? Although it may seem strange that the ancient megalithic wonders were built by us or by our future descendants, we cannot discount it as a possibility.

My current opinion is that these ancient cities were built by ancient humans and that it was done thousands, possibly tens of thousands, of years ago. Is it also possible that at one time the various human ancestors had a shared language, advanced mathematics, and technologies thus were capable of constructing masterpieces of engineering including horrific weapons? If more developed cultures interacted with lesser developed ones, did they share technologies and information? Did this lead to disagreements and conflict? Did they cause a catastrophic event? Could such an event result in eradication of all evidence and memory of such knowledge and technology? Did survivors intentionally forsake and forget their past?

What if thousands of years ago a world war was fought with devastating weapons of mass destruction resulting in equally devastating consequences? Perhaps the people who constructed so many beautiful monoliths destroyed every other trace of ever having been here. If ancient people did rage such a war, is it possible that only their lasting stone creations were able to withstand it? Could it also be possible that it caused the major shifts in Earth's climate that occurred? If they had sophisticated orbital weapons, could they have been enough to alter Earth's axis?

After which, could humanity have gone through a sort of reset? Without the ability to date stone we can only speculate as to the age of these monuments. Some of these ancient cities could be as much as twelve to twenty thousand years old while others may be older. Could there still be more hidden deep within our oceans as much as fifty thousand years old or more? What if this reset was merely one event in a vicious cycle?

Perhaps human beings have been reaching various levels of intelligence only to be reset every few thousand years. What if everything we are doing now has already been done before? We may only be reinventing technologies that our ancient ancestors misused, which resulted in their self-destruction. What if the reason we invent some of these things is because the memories are still there within our genetic code? Could this also be why we find so many ancient creations purposely buried? Did those who buried them do so in an effort to prevent their history from repeating? Did they try to cover up their shame, hide their secrets, and destroy the blueprints for weapons and/or technologies they were unable to control? Or might they have been buried by time, perhaps even continuing over several reset events?

How many times might humanity have undergone a reset? Nuclear wars, floods, meteor impacts, plagues and any number of cataclysmic events may have repeatedly reduced the populations and erased their technology leaving only remnants of once great civilizations and stories that we take for granted as myth. Sudden planetary devastation or drastic climate shifts could explain why some places that seemed to have been tropical were flash frozen in place. Wooly mammoths appear to have been flash frozen while munching on vegetation indicating the freeze was a sudden onset rather than a gradual one. Perhaps there were survivors who managed to live through such devastations by building elaborate underground sanctuaries. Might they have tried to explain what had happened in the past to newly emerging humans through religion and mythology? Might these have been meant as warnings?

Could this be another possible reason for underground civilizations? Might this be the source of global legends concerning underground reptilians or small people? Did a reset event instigate the construction of elaborate cave and tunnel systems? Are ancient civilizations still thriving inside unfathomable caverns? Or is it possible that not only did ancient inhabitants of Earth have the ability to create magnificent monolithic and subterranean cities, but also extra-terrestrial ones?

Instead of other planetary beings coming to Earth in the distant past, could beings have left from Earth and traveled to other planets? What if a prior nuclear war left the planet uninhabitable for thousands of years? Could survivors have left the planet until it became inhabitable again? Were "the gods" returning scouts of a past civilization checking on Earth's progress in preparation for their people's return? Or were the god another entity? Could they have been responsible for resetting humanity?

We have stories of human beings becoming too arrogant and/or gaining knowledge and abilities of "the gods" only to be punished by some calamity. The tower of babel story tells us that all ancient humans all over the world were able to communicate with one another and together build a tower to heaven and that's why they had to be separated and the tower abolished. Might that just mean that the ancient people who were advanced enough to build monolithic cities had perhaps also built something else, a powerful reactor maybe, that caused a reset in humanity? Or could they have created a space program with the intent to explore and colonize beyond Earth making them a perceived threat to other beings in the cosmos?

It's possible that The Ancient Astronaut Theory and my proposed Agar Plate Theory are both accurate. If Homo Sapiens are an invasive species from another planet, might they have gone to war with ancient Earthlings thousands of years ago? Some of Ancient Astronaut Theorists believe Homo Sapiens came from Mars in the distant past due to evidence that Mars once supported life and that the circadian rhythm of modern humans seems to be more in sync with a Martian day than an Earth Day. If an ancient battle took place between advanced Martians and Earthlings, might it have caused Mars to lose its atmosphere and have all but wiped out the cultures of Earth?

Another possibility is that a natural extinction event took place such as the poles shifting or a super volcano erupting. If natural extinction events periodically cleanse the planet of nearly all life, could that explain some of the gaps and variations in the fossil record? Considering how difficult it is for organic matter to become preserved and fossilized in the first place, how much information and ancestry might be missing never to be recovered? Earth is still a young planet, like a teenager with acne, full of volcanic activity with the potential to erase all current life without warning and leave little to no evidence of our ever having been here? We struggle to even predict natural disasters and can do little more than clean up after the fact. Some might say we struggle just as much to prevent war.

Will we inevitably continue this cycle? It may be that human beings, and various other intelligent beings which may have previously existed, can only advance so far in their evolution before a higher power must intervene. Maybe God, maybe Mother Nature, maybe fate, maybe even extra-terrestrials are continually culling our population as we reach our evolutionary plateau. Could be that such resets be necessary for evolution? Each time we are reset, do we leave behind survivors to ensure the evolutionary process progresses? If we are intended to survive and continue evolving into the next group of advanced Earth inhabitants, why all the resets?

Unsustainable

It has long been said that human beings are warlike creatures and that it's in our very nature. Could this be why we can't seem to help ourselves? Even when we are presented with the potential consequences, our hatred for one another almost always wins out over our past experiences and warnings. Could this be the reason for the reset, or possibly many resets, if such a cycle does exist?

Perhaps if a higher sentient power really is intentionally resetting humankind on Earth in the interest of evolutionary progress, it is to eradicate that very nature. If, as the Ancient Astronaut Theory suggests, beings from another world came here and found the indigenous inhabitants to be too prone to violence, could they have intentionally started the process of evolving humanity through genetic manipulation and the culling of the populace? Could they have instigated hybridization between different species and races in order to achieve cooperation and simply eliminated those too violent to coexist with others?

Is it even possible to specifically remove a certain 'nature' from a species? If so, can it be done over several generations through genetic alterations, interbreeding, and pruning? Scientists think they can justify feelings and emotions as well as specific actions linked to them through tangible catalysts such as genes, hormones, and chemicals. Can the feeling we know as rage be blamed on an imbalance? Can the violent actions of

70

an individual be associated with a specific gene? These are some assumptions being made by scientists and studied by doctors with the hope of predicting and possibly 'curing' certain undesirable natural attributes out of us.

What if these attributes, our feelings, which are with us from inception are not dictated by physical catalysts we can study and alter? What if they stem from something beyond us? Perhaps they are a gift to life from the invisible force we refer to as spirit. These gifts we so desperately try to control and/or completely rid ourselves of may be a significant part of what makes up our own human nature.

If, however, a more advance entity has discovered a way to slowly alter the basic natural instincts out of humanity, the resetting of the population on Earth may be vital to ensure that the eliminated traits cannot be passed on to future generations. Near or even total extinctions may be orchestrated to lessen the chances of reemergence.

There are many speculations within this one given rationalization for resetting humanity. While it leaves many opportunities for further speculation and debate it offers little satisfaction for those who prefer simple explanations. A more reasonable conclusion may simply be that the human population is unsustainable. Could populations be reduced whenever the Earth becomes too full and is in need of a cleanse? Might this also explain the extinction of the dinosaurs?

We habitually quarrel over and destroy land and resources. Although human beings are described as social creatures who need interaction with others, we don't seem to tolerate one another well. Conflicts exists regularly even within our innermost circles. There are often clear benefits when large portions of a population are in some way reduced. Could humankind improve from repetitive resets? Some have argued that drastic reductions in human population due to war, pandemics, and natural disasters has been shown to have silver linings. War and pandemics lead to stronger populations, more resources, and an unwillingness to risk further devastation through conflict. Therefore, one could also argue that from such devastation people gain wisdom, tolerance. The reduction in population also creates more room to spread out which means privacy, freedom, and a sense of security. All of this suggests to me that when Earth is over dominated by a species, a reset must and does, eventually take place. Is Earth naturally designed to undergo drastic climate changes every so many thousand years?

If it is as simple as humanity having a propensity for unsustainable population growth, then would the most likely culprits behind the resets be either "God" or "Mother Nature"? Be it through giving us the violent nature that inevitably causes us to war with one another or through various natural disasters the population is reduced enough that life can continue to thrive on this planet. If life were to continuously expand unchecked, would it eventually snuff itself out completely?

There is a balance to everything, and death is essential for the continued existence of life. This is a concept that we as humans seem to have always understood and which can still be found in the Hindi cyclical concept of destruction enabling creation. Maybe some modern-day humans have forgotten as there seems to be an ever-growing interest in extending life, curing all ailments, and achieving immortality.

The current interests in robotics and transhumanization may very well be what leads us to our next reset. Might it have even happened before? Most of us are probably familiar with sci-fi movies themed around machines gaining intelligence, turning evil, and taking over the world. If we were to extend our lifespans by becoming machines, adding machines to ourselves, or building synthetic humans this would likely worsen the issue of overpopulating the planet. Could that alone be enough to trigger a reset? Does the planet somehow sense overgrowth? Does the surface of Earth somehow measure and react to too much pressure from too many life forms triggering a reset?

Another possibility is that there really is a secret organization of "watchers" tasked with keeping an eye on us and resetting us when we reach critical mass. These watchers could be past ancestors, Aliens, Angels, Robots, or even some sort of secret world government. The "watchers" first mentioned in the bible were angels. There are many theories surrounding the existence of "The Watchers" and what their purpose may be. One such suggested purpose happens to be to cull or alter the human population.

If the population is periodically being culled, does that mean humanity is not in fact experiencing total resets? To cull the population would imply leaving survivors. If the population really is being drastically reduced, but not eliminated, why do we also seem to lose our knowledge and advancements as well as any recollection of them along the way? Why are the survivors not passing along our previous histories? Could resets be occurring not to encourage further evolution, but to prevent it? Is humanity being reset every time we advance beyond a specific degree?

Is there a higher being or group of beings preventing humanity from advancing? If so, why? Are resets intended to keep humanity ignorant of our true history? Is there forbidden knowledge that, if acquired, will prompt a global reset? Why should someone, or something, want to keep us from learning our history? What kind of knowledge might be considered forbidden? Is it to protect us, or is it for a more cynical purpose? Perhaps it is to protect someone or something from us. Is humanity so volatile as to warrant being kept in check through periodic eradication?

If the progression of humanity is a potential danger, could the resets be designed to imprison us on Earth? Are we being reset whenever we become capable of interstellar travel? If so, could advance alien entities be responsible for the resets? Are they intentionally inhibiting any possible migration beyond Earth? Are we being treated like a plague which cannot be allowed to escape this planet? Does our unstable nature and unsustainable growth rate make us a threat to the rest of the universe?

What if we were created by a higher being or beings as something akin to bioorganometallic self-replicating machines intended for a specific use? Could we be malfunctioning technology run amuck? Or if Homo Sapien is an invasive species, could interbreeding with native Earth species have exacerbated the aggressive aspect? If highly advanced beings did introduce Homo Sapiens to Earth, whether intentionally or accidently, could they have learned not to repeat the mistake after seeing the planets native species overtaken? Perhaps allowing us to progress beyond this planet would cause detriment to other species and/or other planets.

What if there are higher beings resetting us for more nefarious purposes? Could there be "gods" or a God who doesn't want the beings of this planet to acquire too great a comprehension? If so, is the reason to maintain control over us? Are the resets a means by which to manipulate this planet's inhabitants? Is it to humble us? Is there some truth to humanity gaining too much power and arrogance resulting in divine punishment? Or was it easier for our ancestors to blame it on a higher power rather than admit they destroyed themselves either because they couldn't control their own nature enough to prevent war, or delved into too much power and/or technology too fast? Could some resets have been caused by higher beings while others were intended or self-inflicted? How many times might life, specifically hominid life, on this planet potentially have started over?

Hidden Survivors

Did ancient intelligent hominids suffer complete extinctions only for new species of hominids to evolve and the cycle to repeat? Or did remnants of those who came before us survive devastation and quietly assimilate into newly emerging tribes? Did humanity suffer full resets resulting in a repeat of the entire evolutionary process from microbes in which primates eventually emerged? Or did enough of our genetic information survive to repopulate and advance evolution even further?

Assuming for a moment that at least some portion of the previous population survived, why were they unable or unwilling to preserve their history? Did they attempt to pass on information to their new societies through oral legends and ritual traditions? Did it simply get mistaken for mere myth? Were more recently evolved humans unable to understand? Or have significant portions been misinterpreted and/or forgotten over generations?

Perhaps the survivors felt it was best to forget altogether. If the event or events which ended their advanced civilizations were of their own doing, they may have wanted to erase their history. What if they never assimilated into the newly emerging cultures at all? Could they have decided to go into hiding and avoid interactions with newly emerging societies? Could these survivors have still had some of their previous technology and formed their own refugee camps away from the curious, less advanced new human eyes?

Could some of the survivors have been one of the ancient Pithecus ancestors? If so, might that ancestor have looked drastically different from newly emerging humans? For example, could hairier great ape ancestors have been intelligent, but mistaken for fearsome beast due to a more animalistic appearance? Could some still exist today? If there are still hidden Pithecus decedents, could they be responsible for Bigfoot sightings and such creatures?

Could newly evolved hominids have proven too violent to interact with? Did the newer hominids such as Neanderthal and Homo Sapien wipe out the survivors? Is this why we have ancient stories of our ancestors defeating giants and gods?

This could have led to the legends about gods living among early humans that we find in many early civilizations. There may have been an agreement among the survivors that they would not reveal the truth to these primitive humans. There are stories of certain rebel gods or demigods disobeying the others to share knowledge and technologies with early humans. Could these have been survivors of the past calamity? Could some of the biblical and/or mythological characters and their stories have been real?

There are also stories of the gods interbreeding with humans. If it was the remnants of lost civilization who our ancestors referred to as 'the gods', they may have also been the ones who interbred with our early ancestors. Those remaining from a time before ours may have evolved prior to us and from a genetic line completely independent of ours. This would mean they were genetically similar enough to us to create viable offspring but shared no common ancestry. Could there have been several completely different surviving species? Would that make the offspring formed from such a union hybrids? Could there have been many different hybrids also breeding with one another?

Might some of the legendary beings have been from unique races such as Menehune, Kapa, Tengu, Akua, Twa and others and could they have also been what we think of today as demons, giants, fairies, vampires, angels, elves, mermaids, hobbits, and various other "fantasy creatures"? How do we know that such beings were only imagined? What if some, or even all, of these races existed on Earth? Could any of them still be here hiding in remote locations? What if they're not intentionally hiding? Today with all the different genetic conditions and body modifications we hardly even blink an eye at many of the different attributes of physical appearance making it easier for hidden survivors to blend in with modern society. However, if survivors are not hiding due to appearance but instead due to environmental changes, could their physiology differ drastically from modern hominidae?

Earth may have undergone many compositional changes that we are still unaware of as well as shifts in alignment, temperature, and variations in gravity and electromagnetic fields. Any or all of these alterations could have resulted in a wide range of diverse life forms including significant differences in the many evolving hominids. If the survivors are unable to tolerate the current surface environment due to how much it has changed from a previous time when they thrived, could they be living in caverns, mountains, or even underwater out of necessity? If certain past species did evolve underground and/or in our oceans, could they still be living in those environments? Might that be the reason they were able to survive? Could it be that they are incapable of living on the planet's surface? Perhaps we can only live on the surface due to evolving through hybridization.

The potential hybridization between two hominid species evolving independently of one another may explain rapid evolution over the last few thousand years. Races further along in evolution might have shared genes that others hadn't developed yet. Could hybridization have caused certain new genes to emerge and excel the evolutionary process? For example, could the language gene have developed as a result of two distinct species creating superior offspring? Also, might the genetic memories stored within the DNA of what remained of a previous advance civilization may be responsible for many current inventions? If humanity is experiencing cycles of advancement and destruction, are we also experiencing hybridization between those left over from one cycle and those beginning the next?

When our population reaches a critical point, and we are reset, will some of us survive to then pass on our genome to a new group of recently evolved humans? Will they too think of us as gods? Will our time here on this planet along with all our creations and our history be forgotten as they advance and write their own history? If there were ancient species of humans here before us, is there really no evidence of them left to find? Or has the evidence really been right in front of us all along and simply misinterpreted?

Sizable

It is said that at one time Earth's climate was very hot and humid. During this time period there was a number of very large animals. Those animals have since either gone extinct or evolved into smaller versions over time. These animals are sometimes referred to as megafauna and include Titanoboa, Gigantopithecus, and the famed Megalodon. The age of the Megafauna is estimated to be between 1.6 million years ago to 10,000BC which, if true, would have overlapped with the last ice age estimated to have been between 108,000BC and 10,000BC.

Today we still see similar creatures, though thankfully much smaller, in animals such as the Anaconda and modern constrictors, Orangutans, and various species of sharks. These are just a few examples of giant animals for which we have associated smaller species with today. This suggests that at one time life on Earth may have been gigantic and, perhaps due to the climate cooling, eventually scaled down. It's also possible that Earth had less gravity than it does now if it did go through compositional changes and acquire more mass and heavy metals due to incoming meteors.

What other mega creatures might have existed during this time? Could this be origin of dragons, leviathans, and phoenixes? Did creatures such as these really exist at one time? Perhaps over the years their attributes were exaggerated as the legends were passed on through oral tradition, but could there be some truth to those legends? The Phoenix was said to be able to reincarnate. If a jellyfish can do it, why not a bird? We know that at one time there existed extremely large birds. Could a bird of that size, perhaps resembling today's Cardinal, have been the basis for the many stories and depictions of Phoenixes throughout ancient cultures? If so, perhaps other mythological creatures have origins in the megafauna period.

What does the shrinking of enormous animals have to do with human on Earth? Maybe it simply made the world a safer place for early hominids to start expanding and evolving. Without a landscape full of monsters to keep early humans hiding in caves we eventually became the dominant species. That is one explanation, but again I have another to offer.

There are stories throughout many different ancient cultures about titans, gods, and giants. There's even the Biblical story of the Nephilim. There is also a group of people called the Colossians, the definition for which the Bible gives as being of Colossae. Although I cannot find information pertaining to the size of the church, city, or people, I can't help but notice the similarity between the nomenclature and the words colossal and colossus. Could the city of Colossae have been so named because it was made by giants? Could the Colossians have been giants? Might that be why St Paul sought to establish and maintain Christianity in Colossae? Did he seek to convert and unify all races of the world including beings who may have been hominid species other than Homo Sapien?

What if there's some truth to these accounts? If at one time everything else on Earth was super-sized, why not hominids as well? Could there have been larger human ancestors thriving in advanced megalithic cities during the time of the Megafauna? Could cycles of human civilizations have been emerging and disappearing since as far back as the start of the Cenozoic Era? That would extend our history back to about sixty million years ago. To put into perspective, the current speculated timeline for human ancestry begins between four and seven million years ago potentially with Sahelanthropus, Orrorin, Ardipithecus, or some combination thereof with what we consider "civilization and human history" only beginning about six to twelve thousand years ago. The popular theory still seems to be that civilization began six thousand years ago. If true, what were our ancestors doing all that time?

More specifically, what was so special about the last few thousand years? What are we missing? Evolution takes time, but there is a lot of unaccounted for time in the current assumptions. However, if giant humanoids did create advance cities and were later destroyed leaving only a few remnants behind to adapt and hideout in caves until the planet became more hospitable again, this might account for a chunk of that time.

There may have even been multiple giant hominid species on several different continents. If they were the ones responsible for the various megalithic civilizations all across the globe, they may have been advanced enough to have flight technologies, weapon technologies, energy technologies and global communication technologies that might explain some of the more baffling archeological discoveries still being debated. Some of the oral histories of ancient tribes around the world claim certain structures were built by giants. Why do we simply dismiss those claims?

Perhaps the giants did build those cities and did so as far back as hundreds of thousands of years ago before the last ice age. If there were massive megafauna predators roaming around, might the ancient hominids have needed large, strong stone sanctuaries? If the ancient hominids were giants, it might explain not only the size of the cities and stones used to build them, but also how early humans were capable of building such massive constructs. Could those same giants have taken refuge from the ice age in large caves and underground cities? If so, did they slowly shrink over time and eventually merge with or evolve into another hominid species, like Homo Sapiens?

Also, why do so many people have the misconception that if giants did exist, they were nothing more than violent natured, ignorant brutes? The giants may very well have been the earliest Homo Sapiens or at least one of the contributing ancestors and the very name Homo Sapien means twice wise. I see no reason why giants should be associated with lesser intelligence. That is most likely our own arrogance leading us to make assumptions based more in fictional stories than scientific evidence. It might even go back to the story of David and Goliath or to the Greek Gods defeating the Titans. It was never actually stated that the defeats were due to a lack of intelligence. However, it was implied that arrogance played a role as both defeats were unexpected due to the might of both Goliath and the Titans. If arrogance did play a role doesn't that seem to resemble with modern humans? In my opinion arrogance is often an unfortunate byproduct of intelligence. Perhaps the giants really were the earliest Homo Sapiens and modern Homo Sapien is just smaller, but still arrogant.

One way this can all be interpreted is that the leftover giants did have greater intelligence and technologies, and, in their conceit, they underestimated the new, smaller humans and were thus defeated by them. Another interpretation may be that the conflicts were never between humans and giants, but two different advanced species that had both survived the last reset. This could explain stories of waring gods and demigods. Depictions of many ancient gods, such as Olympians and Anunnaki, appear to show them as being larger than humans.

Another thing to consider is that the giants are often the ones credited with floating monoliths into place to create many of the ancient megalithic sites. There are also stories of the Sitecha who were reportedly giants that lived in floating cities. If they were a superior prehistoric sizable race who were mistaken as the various gods of different cultures, might they have been the descendants of Atlantis? Assuming Atlantis did exist and was a city of high technology, the surviving Atlanteans may have become the Olympians. The gods of Olympus were supposedly the children of the Titans.

Assuming survivors may have established a refugee camp as well as a decree not to interact with the newly emerging humans, could this have caused a civil conflict resulting with the giants splitting into factions and waring with each other? Some ancient legends of certain tribes described their ancestors as receiving help and protection from giants. It may be that a war was fought between those who wanted to interact with humans and those who did not.

If there was such a battle and the victors were those who intermingled with humans, gave us fire and knowledge, and intermarried, then over time they simply would have faded into history as legend. It is believed that Neanderthals interbred with homo sapiens until they disappeared within our genome. Couldn't the same have happened with an ancient, giant species of hominid?

Leftovers or Refugees

The previously posed possibility that there could have been survivors from a past reset of humanity raises a few more questions. Could some of the ancient people who seem to have appeared and disappeared in complete isolation have been leftovers? Could scattered remnants of a lost civilization or cavillations have started over as new ones? Could those 'leftovers' have become the Selk'nam, Ainu, Sherpa, Olmec, Native Hawaiians, Ancient Egyptian, Canaanites and other ancient ancestral societies? Might they all have been survivors from a previous ancient, but advanced Earth?

There do seem to be many similarities between the afore mentioned peoples. Could some, possibly all, have once belonged to the same culture? Several Pacific Island and South American natives, among others, have claimed to be the survivors or descendants of an ancient culture from the Pleiades star system. Many of these same people also claim to be Lemurian. Lemuria is a legendary continent, of which the Hawaiian Islands belonged, that supposedly existed in the Pacific until it became submerged beneath the ocean. Could Lemuria have really existed and suffered a reset? Might the continent have been one super volcano that erupted tearing the land asunder until only the various Pacific Island chains were left? Could survivors of this catastrophe have rebuilt new civilizations based on the same history and culture they shared as Lemurians?

Although we could consider such survivors to be

refugees of the past, there is another type of refugee that may have contributed to our ancestry. Let us assume for a moment that evolved hominids from another planet went out into space exploring, like we are now, and found their way here. They could have been refugees of a dying planet looking for a new home, have crashed here and been stranded, or even just visited and left again.

Many believe not only that we were visited, but that we are still being visited. If that is true, has there been ongoing propagation between those visitors and Earth natives? Is there, as some claim, a hybridization program?

Abductions aside for now, if an evolved hominid from another planet did settle here in the distant past for any reason, might they have been one of our ancestors? If they arrived during a time when the various primates of Earth were not yet developed enough to be of interest, the new settlers of our planet may have left well enough alone and expanded across the globe building thriving stone cities. However, if they arrived during a time when Earth had advanced civilizations of its own, might they have intermingled? Might lonely travelers have sought companionship from the native Earthlings after their long journey through space? Or might we have gone to war?

Are we descendants of refugees, leftovers, or both? Did a humanlike species come here and build an advance global civilization only to be destroyed? Did refugees from another planet come to Earth after destroying their own planet only to repeat their mistakes here? Did indigenous early hominids witness these advance beings create wonderous cities and technologies and then bring about nightmarish calamities? Did survivors and/or visitors assimilate into other civilizations on Earth?

If, however, there were no interplanetary refugees, and the ancient advance beings who built those magnificent cities really were annihilated apart from a few leftovers, are those leftovers also the same beings who created underground labyrinth cities? If there have been multiple resets, each resulting in some survivors, might modern humans have experienced vast evolutionary leaps due to genetic contributions from several previously evolved species?

If some hominid species did evolve underground, could that explain why modern humans are susceptible to sun damage and why we seem to have emerged from caves only to build megalithic walls and structures to hide away in? It is most widely believed that light is a catalyst for life and that life needs light in order to survive, but what if that's not the case? Might light actually be counterproductive to life? Could light be more of a catalyst for death by harming living cells and causing them to decay? Could that explain ancient accounts of longer lifespans? Perhaps if ancient people did evolve underground and slowly emerged, the time spent living on the surface resulted in an increase in cellular damage and aging gradually decreasing life expectancy.

It does seem like biologists discover most new life forms in deep dark places. Could it be because life is continuing to evolve from the darkness even now? Some might argue that the reason we keep discovering new life in those places is due to a lack of previous exploration and new technologies making it possible for us to reach those places. That may be one reason, but it doesn't explain why we don't find as many new species when we reach previously unexplored areas of Earth's surface. There are several dense jungles and rainforest which present their own challenges to reach and navigate through and when scientists are able to investigate new areas they often do find previously unknown organisms, but nowhere near the numbers they find in deep, dark locations.

Could new life be more likely to form in environments resembling the cosmic origin? Earlier I asked if life formed inside of planets and worked its way to the surface over time. If life forms in darker environments and evolves to tolerate light over time, could several or even all of the hominids on Earth have started off in caves or in the oceans? If so, could cellular decay due to living on the surface have been another contributing factor to hominids on Earth dwindling down to one? If living on the surface did lesson the lifespans of other hominids, why didn't they stay underground? Were they forced to the surface by flooding at the end of the last ice age? Did curiosity, lack of food, or lack of breeding partners drive them to seek out other options on the surface?

There may be evidence within our DNA that we are presently unable to comprehend. Maybe we should start considering multiple genetic contributions from previous and/or parallel, but unrelated lines of evolution. We may have genetic information within us from sources beyond our evolutionary timeline or even beyond Earth. As new viruses and microorganisms emerge and start down their own evolutionary paths, are we unknowingly witnessing the seeds of the hominids that will take our place after the next reset? Will there be any leftover Homo Sapiens to influence their development?

Mixing Genetics

Is the human genome hiding a genetic treasure trove of diverse ancestry awaiting discovery? Could modern humans be the result of multiple evolutions from several separate lineages? Could we be the result of interbreeding between similar, but completely different hominins? Will we find the missing chapters of our history within our DNA?

It seems like as we discover more about our genetic makeup in the search for answers, we discover more questions. While we may think we're uncovering explanations geneticists often can only offer speculations. There are those who simply accept those speculations as explanations because they rather have some sort of answer than more questions. It's an infuriating cycle of providing conclusions to satisfy the masses. The anomalies left unexplained are written off as mutations.

Instead of assuming that anomalies are the result of mutations or that there is a "missing link", should geneticists be considering more potential contributors to our genetic information? The possibilities of outside material entering and influencing our DNA from extraterrestrial sources such as new microbials entering our atmosphere should not be dismissed. Furthermore, aren't the notions that all life on this planet evolved from one source, or one location out of Africa just preposterous? Hence my proposed Agar Plate Theory.

I can understand how during the time of Charles Darwin it might've been difficult for people to accept that various multicellular organisms could evolve over time from a common single celled organism more than once, in several locations, and how "the miracle of life" might be a common repetitive occurrence predating even our planet. However, over time human thinking has also evolved and yet we not only accept Darwin's theory as a possibility, but as fact. Why?

In the century and a half since Darwin proposed his theory why has no one expanded upon it by suggesting that perhaps this was not a singular event? The Out of Africa and Multiregional theories may seem like new takes on evolution, but both continue to seek a single original lineage. Why are we not considering parallel, overlapping, and consecutive evolution events? By parallel evolution I mean life evolving from two separate organisms at different locations on Earth simultaneously. By consecutive evolution I mean life evolving from two separate organisms at different times. By overlapping evolution, I mean evolution happening from separate organisms both, simultaneously and consecutively, as well as at the same and different locations. Life may have had an explosion of development across the planet at different places and times which overlapped.

This could have resulted in many different hominins which eventually found and mated with one another. If we are the result of interspecies breeding, what might be the pros and cons of mixing genetics?

Might we have created the language gene by combining the complex genomes of several different humanoid species? Could the reason we appear to be evolving exponentially in more recent years as compared to few thousand years ago be due to the sharing of evolved genetic information or addition of new genetic material entering our bodies from viruses? When we find "new" genes that we are unable to trace or account for are they coming from mutations, viruses, space particles, or simply newly formed from merging genomes? If we are gaining intellectual advancements, what are we loosing?

Some have suggested that even the genetic mixture of two different races in modern times has resulted in new ailments. While it is true that there are some genetic differences between the current races of humanity, we are all considered the same species. So, if mixing the genetics of more than one race has the potential to result in a new genetic disorder, what complications might arise from mixing the genetics of more than one species?

Could this be the origin of disorders like schizophrenia, Fibrodysplasia Ossificans Progressiva (FOP), and Ehlers-Danlos Syndrome? There are many genetic, hereditary diseases that we can't quite explain. Even if we can narrow down which genes are mutated, we don't know the original causes of the mutations. It is assumed that any number of complications during fetal development, exposure to toxins or radiation, or genetic accidents during cell division could've caused mutations that are then passed on to future generations. Would we not be just as likely to see hereditary mutations develop in a species as a result of interspecies copulation?

Are the potential drawbacks worth the advantages? There may be many genetic complications resulting in painful physical deformities, diseases, and disorders as well as psychological ones. We consider the evolution of our brain to be one of our most significant advantages, but is it?

The Brain

The human brain is a complex system that's so delicate the slightest chemical imbalance can cause a plethora of emotions and behaviors. The brain is also so resilient it can overcome unimaginable physical damage and compensate for it allowing continued function. Most people don't realize that even our diets can have a significant impact on how our brains function. Consuming certain substances can cause chemical changes in the brain. Some substances stimulate brain activity while others retard it. Some foods can improve our mood and brain function, protect glial cells and neurons, or have detrimental long-term impact on our mental and/or physical brain health. Mothers who smoke or drink while pregnant alter the development of their unborn child. If one alcoholic beverage can cause fetal alcohol syndrome, what potential affects might the various substances our ancestors consumed have had on human evolution and brain chemistry?

Our genetics determine many of our attributes including intellectual ones. Some illnesses believed to be passed on genetically are Schizophrenia, Alzheimer's, Autism, and Bipolar Disorder, yet diet correlations have been found to worsen or benefit those genetically predisposed to these ailments. When and how did such illnesses originate? Could the brain structure of two hominids separated by a few thousand years of evolution differ significantly? If there's a great enough margin, could the brain chemistries of two species be so incompatible that the brain chemistry of their offspring would be altered enough to create disease? Could that disease then be passed on to future offspring?

In modern science the topic of the brain in relation to a person's race is a highly debated and controversial subject. Every person is unique and every person's brain chemistry is unique. Whether or not there are notable variations between the races should be explored from a purely scientific perspective rather than a racial or political one. However, since modern humans have yet to evolve enough to put aside personal beliefs and hatred for one another, scientists find this subject matter difficult to openly discuss and explore. This exploration should be conducted in the same way we consider correlations between race and diseases like diabetes, without inferring any correlations between race subjective attributes like personality, intelligence, or emotions.

Without enough conclusive information available to determine if there are notable chemical differences in the brains of the known human races, we can only infer that it is a possibility based on the noted genetic and formative differences. None of which is evidence to suggest that the different races of Homosapien were at once prior separate species or each came from a separate ancestor. Personally, I think it would be an exciting discovery to learn that at one point we may have been different species who over time came together to form one. It might mean that our differences, though likely more obvious and plentiful long ago, didn't matter to our ancestors and they coexisted and intermingled until becoming one. Perhaps there's a lesson to be learned from this.

However, so long as human beings nitpick at one another over the differences that make Homo Sapien such an exciting and fascinating species, it will be difficult to explore those differences without the resulting research being misused to fulfill political and, perhaps at times, racist agendas. Unfortunately, this makes me question if we have truly evolved much since the dark ages.

With open minds suggesting that there may potentially be subtle chemical and structural differences in the brains of each race due to possible separate evolutions, could that account for some advantages as well as cognitive disorders? If so, could more notable differences in brain chemistry between two separate species result in more severe adaptations and complications such as hereditary psychological diseases? Are we getting closer to illuminating how and when such benefits and ailments occurred with each generation?

Each time we combine the genetic information of two separately evolved, complex species do we get both significant cognitive capabilities and severe consequences? In order to balance the development of an advantage such as a stronger immune system, might a hybrid offspring develop a disadvantage as well like diabetes. The old saying ignorance is bliss comes to mind. There are several studies suggesting human beings are becoming more depressed due to social expectations, isolation, negative impacts of technology, and a number of other things. While I am all for considering many possible answers, I feel like one big one has yet to be explored. Are people more depressed these days because we are more intelligent?

It is often pointed out that many geniuses suffer from mental illnesses, including depression, and one theory for this is that a higher IQ puts more stress on the brain. The global average human IQ has increased over the generations. If the mixing of species or races led to higher IQ and more geniuses, could it have also taken away the bliss that comes with ignorance, or being less aware? In our pursuit of knowledge, our genetic intermingling, and our natural evolution are our brains under too much strain? Is genetic diversity a contributing factor?

Obviously, I am not suggesting that mixing genetics is wrong or in any way negative. We know that a lack of genetic diversity can cause an array of malformations and weakened or deteriorated genetic information. Genetic diversity is necessary for procreation and good for evolution, but is there a limit? Will the evolution of humanity on Earth eventually plateau? How far can we progress before there is a need for a reset? Would a physical evolution of Homosapien into a new species altogether relieve some of the emotional and psychological strain on our brains? Does the structure of the Homosapien brain need to change in order to withstand the new genetic and chemical combinations? Or do we need to venture out into the cosmos and encounter new species to introduce fresh genetic information into the population?

Consequences

To date, scientists continue to debate what, if any, biological drawbacks we may carry within our genome due to interracial, interspecies, and potentially interplanetary breeding throughout millennia. This controversial notion offers speculatory minds many possibilities to explore. By interbreeding could we be losing previous beneficial traits like the abilities to breath under water and withstand high pressure from an ancestral aquatic or amphibious hominid? However, the proposed possibility of a cycle of resets presents alternate arguments potentially baring similar, perhaps the same, results.

Among the earlier suggested conceivable causes of global resets were war, technological malfunction, and extraterrestrial interference. Annihilation of all hominid life forms on Earth carried out by any of these means could have altered remnant genetic information ultimately changing what new emerging eventual humans became. Resets could have also limited the current human population by eliminating large genetic groups of potentially diverse breeding partners. Could we be unable to evolve further? Are we devolving now? Earthlings, as we are now, may be the result of mutations and limitations caused by our predecessors' eradication.

There are locations where what appears to be evidence of nuclear war in our distant past suggests that the Nagasaki and Hiroshima bombs were not the first of their kind. If ancient civilizations used this type of warfare on one another in a previous cycle, would the resulting radiation have been enough to influence the organisms of this cycle? Could this explain some of our idiopathic mutations? Could radiation from the distant past have altered Homo Sapien ancestors?

Another consideration for total planetary reset is technological advancement beyond mortal control. Did previous civilizations understand technologies that we are now experimenting with, but either were never quite able to stabilize them or intentionally misused them? Could an overload in electromagnetic energy have not only created what is now commonly referred to as Earth's lay lines, but also influenced the way molecules behave? Could experimentation or overuse of electromagnetism and/or frequency have influenced hominid genomes over time?

Electromagnetism has been studied as both a means of renewable energy and as a weapon. Various life forms, including modern humans, have their own electromagnetic field which can be influenced, sometimes heavily, by external forces, even ones beyond this planet. Would an electromagnetic event, with enough expulsion of energy to eliminate life on the planets' surface, have lingering effects on how life forms today?

Could some of the technologies of the ancient past have been living machines, like androids, which utilized frequency and/or electromagnetic energy to perform specific tasks like sanitation, heavy lifting and moving objects, or delivering items and information across great distances? Might such a creation have used the lay lines as a global highway system? If there was a high enough demand for a large number of such creatures, could their creators have made them self-replicating?

John Von Neuman suggested that it would be more feasible to explore space using probes that could create more of themselves from the materials found on the planets they explore. Since then, others have suggested that there may already be such beings in the universe on other planets or even on this one. One aspect of The Ancient Astronaut Theory is that humans on Earth may be self-replicating robots and that we, or at least our DNA, may have been sent to this planet by a more advanced alien society.

What if Homo Sapiens are self-replicating robots, but were not sent here from another planet? What if the species was created by the previous inhabitants of Earth? Did their own creation wipe them out? If so, was it done intentionally as an act of rebellion against our creators? Or did our creation result in their eventual replacement entirely by chance? Could they have made us similar enough to them through DNA technology?

If an advance ancient culture on Earth created what they thought would be "better" versions of themselves, could it have backfired? We are currently creating human-like robots with attributes that we find desirable such as the ability to lift much heavy loads. There is also a desire to have custom, realistic robots made for personal pleasure and companionship. Might this have already been done before? If we were created by a previous civilization on Earth, could they have had a desire to breed with their creation in order to potentially pass on specific attributes to hybrid offspring?

Perhaps that is why we are now all Homo Sapien. Could the planet have been full of a variety of hominids until one of them, or possibly a collaboration, created Homo Sapien? If so, then could this be the reason for why Homo Sapien seems to be an invasive and dominant species? Is being made rather than evolving naturally what lead to the potency of our genome?

Another possibility is that one of the already existing societies of Earth decided to add technologies to their bodies or alter their own DNA in order to enhance themselves. We not only create robots and automated machines, but also artificial devices for our own bodies. Could Homo Sapiens be the result of previous hominids experimentation during their own period of transhumanization? What if changing a seemingly minor trait like pigment in order to get a desired cosmetic benefit resulted in unforeseen adaptations triggered by this unnatural alteration? It might seem like no big deal to change the color of an organism's fur or skin, say from brown to blue, but if it results in that organism being unable to hide by blending into the environment the organism may need to develop a new trait to survive. Could taking away the natural camouflage prompt significant adaptations in order to ensure survival? If so, might those adaptations ultimately lead to a new species all together?

If a past civilization on Earth was experimenting with DNA technology, could they have accidently created a virus, protein, or codon that caused a global pandemic? If so, could they have also used DNA technology to create something to counter that pandemic by altering the DNA of the existing hominids on this planet to be capable of surviving the original mistake? Did this DNA alteration lead to the creation of Homo Sapiens? Or were we the result of the accidental virus, codon, or protein spreading across the globe?

It has also been theorized that an alien society, for any number of proposed reasons, may have reset life on our planet. They may still be periodically resetting evolution on Earth. If there is an advance culture outside of this planet conducting resets, nuclear and electromagnetic are two means by which this can be accomplished. However, another means of resetting a population, which might also result in future genetic consequences, is the introduction of new and potentially detrimental genetic material.

New viruses emerge every year. Most go unnoticed due to their insignificance in our daily lives. Some become pandemics leaving lasting impressions in our memories, and in our own bodies. Viruses are known to alter genetic information and are suspected to be the cause of many mutations.

Microbial organisms can have similar effects on host bodies as viruses. The Black Plague was caused by one such organism. One lasting result was the change in the regions' dominant blood type. The blood type within an individual's body was not changed, but those with the more resilient blood type B became the more prominent among the surviving population. Now what should happen if a virus, to which blood type B is more susceptible, were to spread throughout that population? Could there be secret interstellar travelers introducing illness to slowly, and intentionally, change aspects of our biology like our blood types?

Another aspect of microbial life to consider is that there are specific species afflicted by certain microbial life as though by design. If a virus has a specific host species whose cells are preferable to it chances are that virus won't infect other organism, or if it does the affects won't be as severe as they are in the preferred organism. Instead that virus would likely act more like some parasites who merely hitch a ride on intermediary organisms without infecting them in order to spread to an intended host. If microbes act like those parasites seeking to spread only until they find the ideal host organism, could many of the microbes here on Earth be just passing through? Might they have been traveling the cosmos seeking an ideal host only to have fallen to this planet by chance? What if Homo Sapiens are not the intended hosts even for some of the microbes that do make us sick?

Salmonella is a common bacteria that when ingested can cause a severe case of food poisoning. While it can be deadly in some immunocompromised individuals, in most cases it works its way out after a few days. However, scientists researching how space affects microorganism discovered that salmonella grown under those conditions seems to be as much as three times deadlier. Could it be that Earth is not the ideal planet for salmonella? Could it be that none of the organisms on Earth are ideal hosts for the bacteria? If so, is there a planet with the exact conditions and host preferable to salmonella? Could the bacteria have originated from that planet?

If certain microbes are originating on other planets that support life forms more suited to be hosts, could that explain why some plagues seem to pop up on Earth periodically and then vanish again? For example, could Ebola be mysteriously appearing and disappearing at various times throughout history because it's falling to Earth from space and not finding the type of organism it needs to reproduce and sustain itself? Ebola does infect Homo Sapiens with devastating results, but the fact that it infects and kills quickly is actually counterproductive to the virus. Again, using parasites for comparison, it isn't beneficial to kill the host. Host cells are vital for a virus to metabolize and to spread itself, but Ebola seems to cause too much damage too quickly for Homo Sapien to be an ideal host. However, it would be an affective bioweapon for anyone looking to decrease the population. For that reason, it has been suggested that intelligent beings from another planet may be sending it to Earth as a means to clear the way for their arrival. If there's any truth to that, could intelligent beings, terrestrial or otherwise, have used biological warfare in the past to reset life on Earth?

Just one reset alone could impact our genetic code in several ways. Imagine how remnant DNA and RNA of multiple resets might have contributed to our evolution. Could there be evidence in our latent or junk DNA? Might this be the reason for so many of our mutations and hereditary disorders and illness? Perhaps it was the mixing of trace DNA from the life forms of past cycles, and not the various current races of this cycle, that created so many inherited disorders and defects. Could this be the cause of various physical and psychological illness such as Schizophrenia, Multiple Sclerosis, and some Cancers?

Why would an Extra-Terrestrial society want to reset Earth's population using genetic material? Could Earth be a genetic experiment like some suggest? Or is it simply the most effective way to cull the population of a potential threat to the rest of the universe should humans ever successfully colonize space? Is Homo Sapien DNA so potent that it could become the only remaining hominin genome in the universe, much like it did here on Earth? Could introducing new germs periodically be the best way to both distract and lessen the population? Have some of these occurrences resulted in near, or even total extinctions on Earth in the past?

This would help to fill in some of the evolutionary holes in our human history, but it still doesn't quite answer the questions surrounding the architectural marvels and timeline discrepancies of human civilization.

Even if evolution did occur in multiple locations at different times in our planet's history and new genetic information continually falls to Earth from space, most mainstream scientists still insist that human civilization, began approximately six thousand years ago. Therefore, most sites are dated based on this assumption. They believe that prior to that we were all merely cave and/or tree dwelling hunters and gatherers with only simple tools. There is conflicting evidence which suggests that civilizations may have existed thousands of years before Sumer. Even with this explanation of human development we are still missing a chapter in human history.

Section Four

Ancient Creations

It may very well be that past civilizations simply destroyed themselves with their own creations. Although we haven't found any ancient ray guns or atomic bombs through archeological excavations, we have found evidence of potential nuclear impact and many other peculiar remnants we have yet to explain. We also see evidence of superior technology in the various megalithic structures mainstream science has not explained to satisfactory.

What ancient creations might have existed in a previous cycle of technologically advanced beings? Did they have technologies for entertainment like our televisions and radios? Did they have computers and the world wide web? If they did have something like the internet, could it have existed in a more tangible sense such as a visibly flowing stream accessible throughout various points across the globe? Would such a stream leave behind an invisible, but measurable energy?

This is just one possible explanation for what Alfred Watkins referred to as Earth's ley lines. These lines could be of either natural or artificial origin. There seems to be an increase in electromagnetism at these lines. If they were somehow artificially created and designed to form a calculated grid around our planet, how advanced were the beings who constructed them? They may have been hundreds of years ahead of our current technological understanding. We experienced a scientific and creative setback due to the dark ages in our history, but what if there was a cycle, or cycles, before ours that didn't have such a setback?

There's also the possibility that the ley lines are a natural phenomenon that we may one day better understand and learn how to utilize with increased knowledge in fields like physics and chemistry. Perhaps previous inhabitants, or visitors, of this planet had a better comprehension of planetary ley lines and were able to invent functional technologies from them.

All around the world people have ancient legends of their ancestors building the great monolithic civilizations by "floating" the stones. Whenever the verbal history of a culture is passed down with stories of giant statues or monoliths being levitated into place mainstream scientists are quick to dismiss it as folklore, superstition, and ignorance. It is my opinion that it is ignorant for anyone, especially scientists, to arbitrarily dismiss an explanation just because our current belief system and comprehension assume it to be improbable or outright impossible. Instead, shouldn't we be asking how this was done?

Exploring these claims may provide new insight and inspiration for technologies that turn out to be safer, more efficient, or operate via a renewable resource. Such technologies may have already existed on this planet during a previous cycle. There are common themes among the ancient structures aside from their size, unknown purposes, and mystery. Many of the ancient structures are said to have been levitated into place and/or moved by sound technology. For some reason they also all seem to be constructed from specific stones such as granite, quartz, and basalt. Perhaps these materials were singled out for their unique electromagnetic properties.

There has been some success in laboratories studying electromagnetism as a potential component in anti-gravity technology. Is it possible that the ley lines were used as an antigravitational transportation system to levitate the stones from their quarries and into place? Might that also explain why so many of the worlds ancient megalithic structures are located along specific paths and seem to line up with one another?

Today we have trains that utilize electromagnetism in order to levitate them above their tracks and propel them forward. Could the ley lines have been invisible train tracks? If so, might they have been used to transport large stones from their quarry to intended building sites using floating cargo trains? If these lines were electromagnetic transport tracks, could they have been used by devices other than trains? Another recurring theme in ancient mythologies is that of floating ships. Perhaps instead of levitating trains the ancients had levitating ships which traveled along invisible electro-magnetic tracks.

Another possible explanation for the ley lines is that they supported a type of air travel. Many ancient cultures report flying machines such as magic carpets, vimana, and flying ships. Is it possible that at one time these ley lines produced enough energy to levitate large vessels more than just a few inches? If so, what heights might certain types of machines have been able to reach? Could the lines have produced enough energy to support at least low altitude flying?

Whether or not the ley lines are natural or artificial, they may have been a renewable energy source to power the technologies of a past civilization. Many curious architectural marvels with unknown origins and purposes have been found along ley lines. Such constructs and their possible functions include obelisks, serpent mounds, and pyramids. The Great Pyramids of Egypt are situated in one such position and they are still a hotly debated subject.

The first explanation scientists gave for the building of The Great Pyramids was that they were the tombs of the Pharaohs. There has never been any substantial evidence for this assumption as no mummy has ever been found in a pyramid. Instead, the tombs of the ancient Egyptians are often more like desert catacombs buried deep underground.

Another explanation is that they were ancient power plants. While there has been chemical evidence found in appropriate chambers of the pyramid to support this theory it has not yet been proven and much more study is needed. Even if there is truth to this theory it still leaves many questions unanswered and opens the door for many more questions.

Others have noted that the pyramids align with Orion's Belt and have suggested there is more significance to this than as mere homage to the creation story believed by the ancient Egyptians. Many of the structures from the old world have been found to have astronomical alignments. Several have been described as ancient observatories and star maps. Could The Great Pyramids have been nothing more than a tribute to, and a place from which to observe the constellation of Orion? Could the Ancient Egyptians really have been creating star maps to scale by building their structures at specific locations to mirror the heavens? If so, might they have not only been tracking Orion, but also other stars clusters and their relationships with one another?

An additional theory for the building of pyramids is that it was done either by or for alien visitors who may have been the gods of ancient Egypt. They could have served as beacons or landing pads for alien spacecrafts. Were they modeled after such spacecrafts? Were they meant to represent the benben stone? Were they acting as temporary housing for the gods during their visits? This is another theory that, if proven, could lead to more questions.

I have a few thoughts of my own about what pyramids could be. One such is that the pyramids were built to treat the water being used by the ancient Egyptians, much like our water treatment plants today. The ancient Egyptians claim to be survivors of Atlantis which was reported to have had running water. Egyptians and Romans had flowing water systems to deliver fresh, clean water to their cities and even to public bath houses. The pyramids have been found to have tunnels running underground and connecting them to the Nile. If the ancient Egyptians had a system for pumping fresh clean water from the Nile to their city, couldn't they have also pumped used soiled water from the city into the pyramids?

Scientists have found evidence that the ancient Egyptians had an understanding of chemistry. Could the evidence of chemicals found in specific chambers be due to a water treatment system? Once soiled water was pumped into the pyramids from the city, they would need a way to break down human waste and remove it from the water before returning it to the Nile to be reused. Could that be the reason for having three pyramids and underground tunnels connecting them to the Nile? Perhaps there was a complex water treatment process occurring which provided continual flowing clean water to the Egyptians. If so, did other ancient cultures adopt or have similar systems? Could this be the reason pyramids and other similar structures are found all over the world? Most mainstream scientists believe the mysterious pipes found in a pyramid at Mount Baigong in China to be fossilized tree roots due to how old they are estimated to be, but could they really be left over from a previous Earth civilization?

Another thought that might explain not only The Great Pyramids, but all the pyramids found across the globe is that they may be nothing more than ancient places of worship. If we were to leave this planet or become extinct to be replaced by a group of intelligent beings hundreds or thousands of years later, what would they think if they unearthed churches, monasteries, synagogues, and mosques left behind by us? Some of our places of worship are quite elaborate and built to withstand time. Could all the worlds' pyramids be the places of worship left behind from an ancient lost religion?

What about our museums? We as humans have places in which we store what is historically precious to us as a means of preserving and remembering the past. This practice is not limited by culture or religion. We all have within us a seemingly instinctual desire to leave behind evidence of our existence. Is it because of genetic memory? Do we have stored within us a memory of a civilization that was lost? If there were survivors of previous extinctions, perhaps they left their stories behind in oral traditions and their memories behind in our DNA. Could they have also left behind buildings containing the evidence of the past in pyramids?

We may not have found the physical evidence for this theory because the ancient people of our current cycle happened upon these structures without the presence of mind to preserve or document what they found. However, several ancient peoples did leave behind stories in which they tell of their ancestors finding these places and many go as far as to specify that they did not build them. Some have legends that tell us who did build the ancient structures they found, while others tell us they don't know who built them because their ancestors didn't know. They just happened upon them and made use of them.

Another possible reason for why we've found no definitive explanation inside the pyramids as to exactly what they were used for may be because all potentially evidence literally went up in smoke. Pyramid means 'fire in the middle'. Could the pyramids have been ancient crematoriums? Might the ancient peoples of Earth have all cremated their dead in these magnificent structures in order to send the soul back to the cosmos prior to the belief of souls being able to return to preserved bodies? Or might the pyramids have been nothing more than large braziers allowing travel from one city to another at night?

The ancient Greeks coined the term pyramid which suggest a relation to fire. Pyrrha was the daughter in-law of Prometheus, the god who gave humanity fire, having married his son Deucalion. Deucalion was warned by Prometheus of the great flood, thus he and Pyrrha survived to repopulate the world. Pyrrha is also associated with the color red and many ancient Egyptian structures have been found to have once been painted red.

Red was also the color of protective Egyptian goddess Mafdet. Were the pyramids once painted red? Mafdet does also have a relation to the pyramids in that she was the protector of Pharaohs including Osiris. The Sphinx is exactly opposite the Temple of Osiris at the Great Pyramid Complex and may at one time have also been painted red. If the Sphynx was meant to represent Mafdet and the Great Pyramids meant to represent Orion where Osiris is said to have come from, then the layout of complex may be designed specifically as a physical telling of one of Egypt's oldest mythologies.

If the ancient Greeks saw the pyramids at a time when they were painted red and associated them with their goddess Pyrrha, could they have also mistakenly associated them with fire as well? Or did the Egyptians relate the story of The Benben Stone to the Greeks which they then correlated to the Mythos of Deucalion and Pyrrha? This might also explain why pyramids are sometimes viewed as arks and why Noah's ark has been depicted as a pyramid. In the mythos of Pyrrha, she and her husband survive the flood to repopulate the Earth, much like the story of Noah's Ark. Interestingly enough the Egyptians merely referred to the pyramids as 'mer' which may be interpreted as 'beloved' or 'wisdom' both of which could pertain to the Benben Stone.

Many of the ancients also held a reverence for mountains and volcanoes. Some have suggested that pyramids all over the world were built to represent mountains and/or volcanoes. Volcanoes also have fire in the middle. The Hawaiian goddess Pele was the goddess of fire, lightning, and volcanoes. Might there be an ancient connection between the goddess Pele and the goddess Pyrrha? Could pyramids have been erected to appease fire and/or volcano goddess and therefore built to look like volcanoes? Are they both braziers and places of worship?

If the pyramids are not remnants of ancient church-like or museum-like buildings, did they serve as some other cultural gathering place? Could they have been observatories or places of learning similar to universities? Might they have been used to teach astrology, astronomy, mathematics, masonry, and chemistry? Could they have been places to gather for celebration? Or were they meeting places, like our embassies, to determine important societal and political matters? There are any number of buildings we have today that serve specific roles with which we can compare the potential function or functions of pyramids. We have court houses, pavilions, pharmaceutical and medical facilities, and decorative pieces like the Eiffel Tower that, if found by future scholars of whoever inhabits Earth centuries after we vanish, might be real head scratchers.

My thoughts on the pyramids do tend more towards the idea that we are seeking a profound truth for something quite simple and ultimately meaningless to us beyond mere historical value. I realize suggestions such as the pyramids being water treatment facilities or mere churches may not equate to the mysterious and meaningful explanations some may be hoping for. However, I do have some thoughts which, if true, would provide greater justification for continued exploration of pyramids worldwide.

If the pyramids were advanced pieces of technology used by ancient civilizations, might they have powered the various legendary flying machines of the ancient world? One speculation is that the pyramids were producing hydrogen gas. If true, could they be providing the hydrogen gas for flying machines like zeppelins? Could ancient technology have inspired the invention of the Zeppelin? German scientists were known to have researched ancient cultures. Is it possible that the stories of vimana in Hindi culture, the Magic Carpets of Persia, and the various flying ships of other cultures including Japan and Egypt were all describing Zeppelins from a past civilization or civilizations of Earth? Or might the ancients have had much more sophisticated technologies than mere Zeppelins?

If at one time the various civilizations on Earth were advanced enough to have nuclear technologies, including atomic weapons, could they have gone to war with one another and essentially causes a global nuclear reset? If so, perhaps what survivors remained built structures to clean up the nuclear waste in the form of pyramids. Could the pyramids have been built as a last effort to restore a devastated Earth's atmosphere? Did the various pyramids all over the planet produce atmospheric gasses via chemical reactions? Perhaps this was done thousands of years ago. Could pyramid complexes all over the world have provided housing and protection for the survivors who stayed behind to monitor and maintain the process?

Did the survivors leave the uninhabitable planet in search for a temporary home while the pyramids were left to reestablish Earth's climates and ecosystems? If so, have they been watching Earth from afar? Did they return? Could this be the explanation behind the UFO phenomena? Did they leave behind any records of their history for future generations to find so the same mistake wouldn't be repeated?

Could the pyramids and potentially even other ancient megalithic sites have been built as fallout bases for the survivors to live and work from? Did they create these sites as natural filtration systems to aid in the planet's recovery? Perhaps that's why specific types of stone and materials were needed. Could that also be why those ancient civilizations seem to have died off? Perhaps many survivors fled to space or to underground cities, but volunteers remained on the surface to create and manage the facilities needed to undo the damage. If so, did living in and working from those sites result in long term exposure? Did those volunteers sacrifice themselves for the remaining survivors and the future of this planet?

Could the reason pyramids are sometimes depicted or described in ancient cultures as arks is due to legends like the Benben Stone, Deucalion and Pyrrha, and Noah's Ark be because there is some lost truth to these tales? Might there have been pyramids for each ancient culture's chosen survivors to wait out a devastating flood? If so, how were the survivors of each culture chosen? Were some selected based on skills and future needs? Were lotteries held? Could some of the sites have been created to house and protect other life forms of the planet? Could volunteers have gathered and tended to various plants and animals they wished to preserve? Or might they have had DNA banks similar to our Frozen Ark Project and our seed banks of today? Perhaps the reason we haven't found any evidence stored DNA is because it was all reintroduced to the planet over time.

If it is true that at one time the ancient people of this world destroyed everything by means of nuclear war, do our current world leaders know? Could our governments be keeping this from their people to avoid causing fear? Perhaps the truth was discovered during World War Two when Hitler had his Nazis looking into the rumored weapons of ancient cultures. If this was how the scientist of the time were able to develop nuclear capabilities, did they not fully understand the potential planetary devastation? Was this something we had to learn for ourselves only after witnessing the worldwide radioactive consequences of using such weapons?

Or could our governments have known that this happened in the ancient past and be keeping it secret out of shame for repeating the same mistake? Could they also be concerned that sharing whatever they may have learned contradictory to current historical and religious beliefs would cause global social and political chaos?

If a past civilization wanted to preserve knowledge

and knew better than to leave behind writing and objects vulnerable to the corrosion of time, could they have erected suppositories for future inhabitants or visitors of Earth to find? Could some of these suppositories have been historical libraries containing the art, music, literature, math, and histories of past cultures? Could others have been laboratories storing chemical, genetic, or industrial data on technologies developed within them?

If the pyramids are ancient suppositories containing the knowledge of people who lived on this planet prior to a reset, could there have been beings from later resets who discovered and added to the suppositories? Could each pyramid be a suppository added just before a reset to represent a specific culture of that cycle? Will we later contribute by adding our own suppository in the form of a pyramid? If so, will it be one pyramid representing all of humanity, or will it be a pyramid for each unique culture of our cycle's history?

Why leave knowledge in such a puzzling form as a pyramid? Was it to grab the attention of future inhabitants? Did they assume the size and shape of such structures would be recognizable symbols? Could it be due the properties of the materials they're made from? Perhaps they needed the longevity of stone and their specific skill in masonry to ensure the survival of the structures. If the lifespans of ancient people were hundreds of years, it makes sense that they would want their structures to endure. However, could the materials chosen have also served another purpose like storing information? If the information stored was intended to be accessible for millennia, was the type of stone chosen necessary to prevent that information from being lost?

Earlier I mentioned the electromagnetic properties of

quartz and basalt when focusing on antigravitational technologies, but there may be another reason for choosing quartz to build ancient structures. Quartz can be used to store massive amounts of data. The pyramids are not the only ancient structures with the potential to have been built as a means of storing the knowledge of past societies, either from Earth or just visiting. Obelisks are equally mysterious and can also be found all over the world. Could they be ancient suppositories as well?

Just as with the pyramids, I have some thoughts of my own about what the function of obelisks might've been. Thinking back to the ley lines as potential streams of energy, might they also be streaming information? Could obelisks have been erected at specific points on lay lines to act as servers? Perhaps they were intended to both store and share information between them.

Obelisks are large stone towers, typically made of quartz or basalt containing quartz, with the potential to store or transfer energy and/or data. Could they have been communication towers? I'm not suggesting there were cell phones, at least not in any recent cycle of history, or we probably would have found an artifact that in some way resembled a technological device we could associate with long distance communication. Mind, that is a suggestive statement and there may be a misunderstood, misidentified metal artifact thought to be a tool or weapon of ancient times in a museum right now that is actually a fragment of previous phone-like technology.

However, presumptuously continuing my original examination of obelisks as communication towers, could they have transmitted rhythm or even sound? Could the obelisks have been used for transmitting or amplifying sound across great distances? Might they have been radio broadcasting towers? Perhaps they carried recognizable sequences of pulses from one point to another. We used a series of beats in morse code to relay messages across the globe in a time in our history that we might look back on today as being rather primitive.

Evidence of the use of sound as both a form of communication and as a technology has been found in many prehistorical locations. Mayan temples, underground cities, and Hindu columns have incorporated sound into their structures with remarkable precision. Sound is known to have a profound influence on both our physical and metaphysical selves. Practices passed down through some cultures for thousands of years indicates that ancient people understood sound in ways we may have forgotten.

Could obelisks have been used to transfer sound waves? If so, would they have been merely vibrations with specific intent, such as a recognized frequency as a code like our morse code, or could the actual voices and words of people have been carried over great distances? Did people speak to one another through obelisks? Perhaps they used the electromagnetic properties of the quartz to produce radio waves. It might have taken some time to communicate this way depending on how it was done, but from studying the astronomical correlations of ancient structure we can extrapolate those ancient civilizations were both patient and meticulous. This might also explain how the different ancient peoples of the world seemed to be in regular contact with one another without flight.

Or if they did in fact have flight, perhaps obelisks served in some way as flight towers. If the ancient civilizations did have vimana, zeppelins, flying carpets and so on, it stands to reason that they may have needed flight towers. Could they have been a means of lighting the way along ancient flight paths at night? Could they have acted as boosters to charge or enhance the energy of the ley lines if they were used to levitate trains or ships?

Another possibility is that if the ley lines were created, the obelisks were a key component in their creation. Perhaps the ley lines as we know them now are nothing more than residual energy left over from a system created by the obelisks. What if some energy is still being produced at ley lines is due to the piezoelectric effect from the quartz within structures still left standing upon them in spread out locations?

They could have been something akin to electrical towers. What if the obelisks were a constant renewable source of energy powering the globe by means of absorbing solar or kinetic energy from the wind and converting it to electrical or electromagnetic energy and transferring it down the line? We convert kinetic energy from wind turbines and dams into electrical and transfer it without losing any by means of alternating currents. Could obelisks have been ancient sources of power using a similar method?

Another debated ancient creation out of Egypt is the Serapeum of Saqqara. While it is said to be a sacred burial place for Apis bulls, there were no bull mummies found in the sarcophagi. Also, the size of the sarcophagi, the material from which they made, and the precision of the craftmanship warrants further inquiry. How were they made? How were they moved? Who was responsible? Why go through all the trouble?

Assuming for a moment that there was an ancient civilization here on Earth, they were of giant proportion, and they did create large and precise stone works, could they have created the sarcophagi? Also assuming that there was an atmospheric concern on Earth due to nuclear war or some other devastation and the ancients did create pyramids and leave behind survivors to resolve the issue, could those sarcophagi have been used for healing purposes? Might they have been something akin to a hyperbolic chamber? Did the ancients know how to use frequency and electromagnetism to heal the body inside giant stone chambers such as the Saqqara sarcophagi? Might they have been stasis chambers intended to sustain the survivors while they waited in rest to see if their restoration of the atmosphere had been a success? Or might they have been specially designed to hold the bodies of anyone who succumbed to radiation poisoning due to nuclear fallout?

If the sarcophagi did contain giant advanced beings in stasis and the Ancient Egyptians found them, might they have awakened? If so, could the Egyptians have mistaken this as the dead returning to life? Perhaps this is why the Egyptians mummified their dead. What if those beings stuck around for a while before leaving and taught the Egyptians about medicine, chemistry, mathematics, astrology, astronomy, metallurgy, and masonry? Could they have been the beings the Ancient Egyptians referred to as their gods? Instead of having come from Orion, might those beings have left Earth and gone to Orion? What if the Ancient Egyptians were not the only culture to have encountered survivors of a past reset? Or could they have been the survivors? It may be that due to pasts cataclysms and resets knowledge was simply lost and forgotten over time.

If ancient Earthlings did survive a reset event by escaping into the cosmos, could they have left behind devices with which to monitor the conditions of the planet for future return? Might that be why some objects in our orbit appear to be artificial despite seemingly not belonging to any current Earth nation? Could the same be said for some of the NASA moon and Mars photos that have been debated? If an ancient Earth culture built magnificent cities, air and space craft, and various other unknown technologies before leaving the planet, might they have also built satellites?

There have long since been rumors of something orbiting Earth before modern nations launched their satellites. Some ancient cultures described a bird or seat of their god or gods circling the planet. Even some scientists have speculated over the years about a possible hidden satellite predating our first recorded launch. As far as anyone today knows, the first satellite launched was Sputnik in 1957. What if the rumors of a preexisting satellite are true? Instead of assuming if it's not ours it must be aliens, might it have come from a previous Earth civilization?

If there was a global even causing the ancient civilizations of Earth to flee into the cosmos, could they have known about their impending doom in time enough to collaborate and build a special city and departure base? If so, could their point of departure be what is now the ruins of Puma Punku? Could the nearby city of Tiwanaku have been built as a commemorative city of all the races of Earth? Perhaps Puma Punku was created as nothing more than a lunch site for large vessels designed to support life through a long pilgrimage into space. If large groups of people were being carried to safety aboard such space craft in an organized manner the city of Tiwanaku may have also been a prelaunch gathering place.

If not a gathering place for refugees from various ancient Earth cultures to prepare for departure, might Tiwanaku have been a lab? If the ancients created android like beings to tend to the planet in the hope of one day returning, could Tiwanaku be the place where such beings were created? Might those beings have been one of our ancestors? Was there an ancient Earth civilization that left the planet from what is now the ruins of Puma Punku and leave behind clues for us to find at the nearby city of Tiwanaku?

If that same civilization possessed knowledge and technologies far beyond that of current nations what else might they have created in the solar system? Just as there are stories about potential satellites dating back into antiquity, there are also legends about how the moon came to be. Many cultures have recounts of the moon being created and put into position or brought here from another location. Could there be some truth the notion that Earth's moon might be an artificial and intentionally placed construct?

There is much speculation today concerning the exact composition of the moon and whether it is hollow. Many theories attempt to explain its formation, but some have pointed out the convenient size, position, and magnetic effects of the moon seem to indicate intention. Assuming the moon is an artificial creation precisely sized and placed to achieve ideal living conditions on Earth, how was it done?

Could the creation of the moon have something to do with all the basalt and granite spheres we find around the world? The moon is more or less just another mysterious basalt sphere. Perhaps there were several civilizations on Earth with knowledges and technologies surpassing are own. If so, did they work together to solve global concerns such as meteor threats, atmospheric erosion, and tumultuous climate conditions? Might the creation and placement of the moon have been a global collaboration implemented to solve all of these issues and improve living conditions on the planet? If several advanced ancient nations worked together to construct the moon, could all the mystery spheres across the planet be evidence of this endeavor? Perhaps the spheres are different prototypes left over from the various ancient cultures involved. Could that explain why they come in a variety of sizes and why they are made of igneous rocks with magnetic properties?

Were several different civilizations of ancient Earth forced to come together to create and precisely position Earth's moon? Did the survival of life on this planet depend on it? It has also been suggested that settlers from another planet are responsible for the moon. If Homo Sapiens are an invasive species originating from Mars, could they have come to Earth seeking refuge due to the loss of atmosphere? If so, instead of warring with ancient Earthlings, might they have collaborated with the advanced civilizations here in order to prevent the same thing from happening to this planet? Could the many skulls displayed at Tiwanaku represent the various peoples who came together to accomplish this task?

Or if ancient Earthlings did leave the planet due to devastation and were capable of creating advanced technologies in the form of megalithic structures, could they have created the moon as part of the atmospheric restoration process? Perhaps the pyramids were designed to eliminate toxic gasses and/or radiation and reintroduce a livable atmosphere while the moon was designed to protect the new atmosphere from radiation, erosion, and bombardment of meteors. Perhaps both the moon and the asteroid belt can be explained by this. What if instead of constructing a moon from scratch, an uninhabited planet was chosen and destroyed in order to harvest its core? Might the asteroid belt be left over debris from a planet intentionally demolished for this purpose? The asteroid belt is close enough to potentially relocate a planetary body into Earth's orbit.

If the moon was created as part of an elaborate planet sustaining system, could Earth's Van Allen belts be an intentionally designed part of that system? Or are Earth's Van Allen belts just a beneficial happenstance? Could an ancient Earth civilization have understood cosmic energies and workings to the extent of not only being able to manipulate planetary conditions and potentially create a moon, but also to design and position everything in, on, and orbiting the planet such that every ideal condition would be met?

Assuming that the ancients did possess technologies to alter or potentially even create planets, could they have also designed smaller pseudo solar systems here on Earth during times of need? For example, during the period when it is believed that a catastrophic event caused ash to rain from the sky and block the sun, could civilizations surviving underground have created their own pseudo sun? It is difficult to imagine large populations sustaining for extending periods of time without a light and heat source.

In some archaeological locations excavations have uncovered various balls and disks made of gold or mica. Both gold and mica are superconductors capable of providing light and heat while also providing protection from radiation in the event that the cataclysm was brought on by nuclear war. Might we be looking at ancient nuclear fallout bunkers lined with gold and mica to provide sustainable energy and radiation protection? There are also ancient legends of revered sun disks. Could these disks have been so cherished because they acted as replacements for the sun during a literal dark period?

When we consider how much the different cultures

from six-thousand or more years ago seem to have understood about astronomy, masonry, electromagnetism, math, and sound, why would anyone picture them as ignorant? From my perspective they appear to have been far more intelligent than mainstream scientist would have us believe. They may have also been wiser than humanity as a collective is now due to the discipline required to master those subjects through self-study, apprenticeships, and continued practice. Have we lost a great deal of knowledge, wisdom, and skill due to our faster, more readily available technologies and easily accessible databases? Do we find it hard to believe ancient people had advance, possibly even superior, technologies because we now lack the understanding and imagination of our ancestors?

What other technologies could our prehistory have kept secret? Did these secrets have to come from higher evolved beings from another planet, time traveling, prior advancement and extinction, or gods? Could the explanation be as simple as human beings having existed for longer than we think and having had superior knowledge and technologies we are unable to understand? Did a tumultuous history of human emotion, destruction, hubris, apathy, and attrition slowly erase chapters of our past? How much of ourselves have we lost along the way?

Ancient Knowledge

Could some of what we consider to be myths, decorative art, primitive tools and weapons, and ritualistic eccentricities have been our scholars and scientists misinterpreting and often outright discrediting what our ancestors tried to teach us? We make assumptions about when writing was developed based on our limited understanding of surviving texts, but what if there existed an ancient form of communication that we have yet to identify as a written language simply because we are too far removed? It is difficult enough for us to recognize the structure and attempt to translate languages from just a few thousand years ago. What if there is evidence of advance communication from several thousand years ago all over the planet that escape our notice because we are unable recognize as language?

We also assume our ancestors knew nothing of chemistry because of the Faux-Pas of alchemy like mistakenly consuming mercury. Yet without the alchemy of the time, we may have taken much longer to rediscover chemistry. I say rediscover because evidence shows many ancient civilizations had varying understandings of chemistry. If the dark ages hadn't set us back, how much greater would our grasp of chemistry be now? Then again, could the dark ages have bought us enough time to evolve emotionally enough to handle atomic weapons?

Considering we weren't evolved enough not to use

them in our cycle, or not to make them in the first place, one could argue that no matter the cycle or level of evolution we simply can't comprehend the devastation without living it. Thus, with or without 'dark ages' slowing human progression, weapons, advancements in weapons, and the use of those weapons are all inevitable. There's also an argument to make about human nature which may not apply to previous cycles if those beings were something other than human and if their extinction was caused by something other than war.

Philosophical arguments aside, it is likely we can add chemistry to our ancient ancestors list of well-studied and intricately understood disciplines. In that list archeologists already include math, not only because it is essential for the other studies, but also because there is another relic of the ancient world that may have been misinterpreted as a geometric marvel. It's true that Mandalas can be considered geometric works of art, but they are described by many cultures as having spiritual significance as well. It is also possible that mandalas were the means by which the vimana were flown. If the mandalas represent different sounds, could the specific patterns of each mandala depict the exact tone needed to levitate specific vimana? The mandala is also said to be a two-dimensional representation of the universe which is said to have its own sound.

If mandalas show the cyclical nature the universe, our world, and ourselves and are considered a depiction of the cosmos, could they also contain knowledge in other disciplines? Some scientists have associated them with ancient peoples' study of geometry. However, what if it isn't so much about math and astronomy, but more about cosmic relationships right down to the molecular level? Perhaps the important connections between Mandalas and astronomy are mysticism and chemistry.

Chemistry is just as important to the cosmos and to creation as physics, if not more so. Today we place so much importance on the studies of Math, Physics, and Biology when trying to understand our universe and ourselves that Chemistry often feels to me as though it's an underappreciated, and under taught subject. Perhaps we don't know Chemistry's true value because we have forgotten. Did ancient people draw complex, detailed dodecahedral representations of the cosmos because they were trying to tell us something about molecules or a specific molecule?

Although there are currently no known naturally occurring dodecahedrons, could the mere shape be a clue? Perhaps the first Mandala was drawn as a two-dimensional representation of a dodecahedron. If so, why use it to depict the universe? Another heavily debated topic is the shape of our universe. Opposing the controversial Holographic Universe Theory suggesting a two-dimensional universe, which would also suggest 'flat', is the suggestion that the universe is either spherical or oval. Some have referred to it as 'egg' shaped. Do we find it easier to accept a spherical, oval, or egg-shaped universe due to our own perceptions or subconscious ideals? Or is there some remnant of the knowledge our ancestors had about the universe that has been buried within us for so long we have forgotten the significance of dodecahedrons? Perhaps it's two-dimensional and twelve-sided making it a dodecagon instead.

Great minds through-out our history as far back as Plato theorized the Earth may be a dodecahedron. As a child I consistently drew planets as dodecagons because something about it just looked "more right" to me, even though teachers made every effort to remind me that Earth is round. Globes that are perfect spheres still seem a bit off to me, while soft rounded dodecahedral globes just feel right.

As a child I was unable to offer an argument beyond my preference in the appearance, but the first time I saw three-dimensional models of molecules it started me asking more questions about Chemistry than any other subject. It would turn out that of the many questions I would ask teachers, and later college professors, the questions for which they had answers were most often the ones pertaining to Math, Physics, and Biology. Many of my questions had a lot to do with molecules and compounds and their interactions. For those, answers were often scarce or lacking. Did our ancestors draw Mandalas to represent the structural rule of creation?

In our current understanding of chemistry, we believe a dodecahedrane can only synthesized in labs and has no molecular significance besides symmetry. However, we have made incorrect assumptions in chemistry before. Elements and structures we thought impossible were later discovered or made in a lab. Perhaps Plato had a reason for being interested in polyhedrons beyond their geometric shapes. Could he have come across an ancient reference for a specific substance or element having both great cosmic significance and a dodecahedral shape?

If ancient people once possessed a comprehension of Chemistry such that they could determine molecular shapes, did they also figure out how to reconfigure substances? It is possible that the idea of our world and universe being dodecahedral came from their stone masonry skill. Perhaps in perfecting their building technique by creating aesthetically pleasing and architecturally gratifying structures such as stupas, an epiphany was born that this must be the supreme shape. However, the most ancient writing we have on Mandalas does not specify that mandalas represent stupas or great feats in stone masonry, but that they depict the cosmos. Could mandalas have been something akin to ancient blueprints for megalithic architect?

If the concept of drawing a dodecagonal layout of the universe was derived from a disciplined study of Chemistry, how was that mastery achieved? Did our predecessors have a means to view compounds and a way of observing interactions between them at the molecular scale? Was it the same means by which their stone masonry and exorbitant alignments were so precise? Did it also allow concoctions to be made for poisons, medications, weapons, and other chemical tools?

In many ancient writings there are mentions of weapons like liquid fire, elixirs of lasting youth and immortality, and the infamous Philosopher's Stone that transmute one substance to another. Could the Philosopher's Stone have been just a name of a tool used during a specific chemical process? Could it have been a crystal or lens that enable microscopic magnification? Instead of a single stone, could it have been a type of stone that when crushed and heated produced an even greater temperature which allowed them to manipulate elements with higher melting points?

How many of the chemical achievements of the ancient world were merely accidental discoveries of trial and error? There is evidence from long extinct civilizations all over the world indicating they knew what ingredients they needed, where and how to find them, and by what process to combine them. What if the ancient people knew more about chemistry than we do? The ancient Greeks had a weapon described as liquid fire which burned even in water. Did they know how to make Thermite?

Thermite is a powder made from aluminum and metal oxide which causes an exothermic reaction. Theoretically, if the ancients experimented with mixing different ground metals, including rust, they could have figured out that a thermite mixture would burn hot enough to melt granite and potentially have used that knowledge to soften and shape stones to fit perfectly together. There are some ancient accounts of something being poured on the stones in order to mold them.

Another ancient Greek compound described as either the food or the drink of the gods was called Ambrosia and was said to bestow longevity, possibly even immortality. Was this the substance responsible for some historic figures having been reported to have lived for several hundred years? If it was described as both a food and drink, was it something like a smoothie or pudding? Or was Ambrosia a meal consisting of two substances that had to be consumed together? Was this a recipe invented from an intricate knowledge of biochemistry?

Could they have even understood the importance of electrolytes and organometallic compounds in our bodies? Might that be why Ambrosia had a red color to it? Did it contain the organometallic compound we refer to as B-12? Could ancient people simply have found and ingested red cinnabar, cobalt, and chromium containing compounds? If so, could this be due to the assumption that such compounds were related to blood and life due to their color?

Could other ancient geometric designs associated with spiritual practices have actually been two-dimensional representations of compounds? Could these have been the precursors to Lewis structures? Did some of these even get adopted by later religions as spiritual symbols? Were the pictograph type symbols later used in the alchemy of our more recent history due to the knowledge of ancient chemistry and molecular structures having been lost? Or were alchemists of the time aware of the ancient knowledge, but forced to write in code and secrecy under religious control? Was all previous knowledge and recollection of ancient chemistry lost until the rediscovery of alchemy?

If mandalas and other ancient shapes left by past civilizations are representations of geometry, could they have been trying to simplify their advance mathematical concepts for future residents of Earth to comprehend? Should we be looking at these shapes through a larger academic scope to encompass physics, music, astrology, and chemistry? Perhaps these shapes are meant to be deciphered using all fields of study. Many scientists, including archeologists and anthropologists, believe that we are more intelligent than humans in the past. They believe we discovered the modern concepts of math and physics, and that thousands of years ago people were far less sophisticated.

What if we are only just now rediscovering concepts that ancient Earthlings had mastered? What if our current understanding of these various fields of study doesn't even come close to that of ancient cultures? Are there fields of study we still haven't even discovered? Do we dismiss some ancient studies as superstitions, fanciful practices, spirituality, and misinterpretations? Perhaps we are the ones misinterpreting. Astronomy is one study in which we seem to be considerably lacking in comparison with people of the ancient past. However, at least it is considered a science about which we are trying to learn more unlike Astrology. To most, Astrology is severely misunderstood as superstition or a joke despite the number of people all over the world regularly checking their horoscopes.

What if there is a lot more to the study of Astrology in which ancient civilizations were well versed? Does the constellation under which a person is born have some role in that person's individual electromagnetic field? Should we consider Astrology from a more open minded and scientific viewpoint? Could studying Astronomy and Astrology together as one help us to better understand both the universe and planet Earth? Should we consider Astrology to be another sub-study of Astronomy much like Astrophysics? Perhaps the ancient people of Earth did not distinguish between these studies and were therefore able to understand more by looking at the bigger picture.

Could the different ages, such as the age of Aquarius we are now in, actually have a more profound meaning that has been lost to us over the millennia? What significance might there be in astrological ages? Were there different ways of measuring time prior to ones we know of from more recent past cultures? Were the astrological ages relevant to past concepts of time? If so, could exploring these concepts lead to scientific revolutions?

Did they also incorporate music into their study of the cosmos? Could that be why they seem to have had a higher understanding of frequency and sound technology? We are only just beginning to concede the importance and possibilities of sound. Did ancient cultures use frequency to levitate and move monoliths as they claim? Could it have been a combination of frequency and electromagnetism? Did they not only have a higher understanding of sound, but of other energies such as gravitational, magnetic, and even photonics? Did they study the energies of both Earth and the cosmos? Could they have had a far more advance understanding of physics? Perhaps they didn't study "physics" at all. Could their spiritual studies of energies have given them a more complete understanding of what we call physics?

We tend to think of physics in terms of math, but perhaps the combination of Astronomy and Spirituality provided ancient people all the understanding of the various energies and how to use them. It is entirely possible that even their understanding of advance mathematical concepts came from this. Not all of us are able to view and learn math from a linear perspective. I, myself, understand mathematical concepts through art and music. Perhaps the past inhabitants of Earth used sound to understand shapes and measurements. Could music give us a more complete understanding of concepts we categorize as theoretical math and physics? Were ancient people actually studying and utilizing energies which we know today as phonon and photon energies?

Perhaps some ancient terminology has been misunderstood. Many people understand magic to be a mythological practice of manifestation from spells and conjurings. What if magic was instead the manipulation of unseen energies, either instinctual and unintentional or directed by someone well practiced? Could ancient Earthlings have been more in tune to natural energies and better able to utilize them? Could they have understood how frequency and light interacts with matter and learned to manipulate those energies?

If an ancient culture once manipulated light and sound, could they have created technologies that used and manipulated phonons and photons? Phonons actually have negative mass and seem to repel gravity rather than be pulled towards it. When we consider the various ancient accounts of levitating stones using sound technology, the unusual properties of phonons becomes far more intriguing. How might better understanding those properties allow us to potentially achieve the same antigravity technologies the ancients may have possessed?

Why stones? Could it be that the crystalline materials in stone, especially basalt and granite, make them ideal for light and/or sound technologies? Might there have even been technologies specifically designed to alter and/or influence those crystalline structures with a purpose? Did those technologies simply make the stones lighter and easier to move? Or were there technologies that enabled precise cutting and shaping of stone?

If the ancients understood how to manipulate light and sound energies to create advance technology and magnificent megalithic stonework, could they have discovered how to use those energies to alter the perceived physical world? Might they have discovered interdimensional travel, time travel, or even long-distance space travel? Could they have devised a stable method of creating and maintaining wormholes? Did they not only understand the natural world on a molecular level, but on a sub-particle one as well?

If people in the distant past did have an advance comprehension of chemistry and energies, did they also have an advance comprehension of biology? Could they have practiced medicine far beyond our own? Did they use specific knowledge and technologies to assist or accelerate the body's natural healing process?

If they were somehow aware of chemical and biological compositions and processes on a molecular level, could they have known what foods and substances to consume for medicinal purposes? Did they collect certain materials for mixing compounds? Could they have also mixed potions and elixirs for increasing vitality? Might this explain the apparent longevity of some ancient, alleged rulers?

Were some of these compounds intended not to heal ailments or prolong life, but to enhance particular attributes? Did they intentionally alter body and brain chemistries to achieve specific physical sensations, mental clarity, psychological stability, and altered perceptions?

What role might their potentially advanced knowledge of energies have played in medical practices? Some ancient structures seem to have been designed to reverberate sound at a precise frequency. Were these structures medical chambers? Today we have hyperbaric chambers which use Oxygen to treat or heal different ailments. If the ancients did possess sound technologies might this also be where we get the ideal of spells? In many ancient cultures and even in the religions of today we are aware of "the power of the spoken word" and we associate magic and spells with words and/or chants. Might there have been ancient chants or even songs devised to resonate at desired frequencies for specific purposes including healing? Did ancient Earthlings use resonating chambers to produce different intended effects on the body?

Could there also have been other medical structures designed to use other energies to impact the body in distinctive ways? When exploring ancient structures, should we be looking for anomalies involving energies such as gravitational, magnetic, electrical, electromagnetic, piezoelectric, thermal, radiation?

Perhaps some of these ancient practices can explain stories of shapeshifters. Any substances designed to alter perception could also be used to create convincing illusions. Some substances have such powerful influence over the mind that they can be used to provoke hallucinations or plant false memories. For example, scopolamine can be used to manipulate a person's behavior and memory. Therefore, it is possible that some stories of shapeshifting were merely elaborate acts of psychological warfare and manipulation. What if druids, shaman, alchemists, and medicine men of some ancient cultures learned how to use substances to make others believe they could shapeshift? Perhaps this is also why wearing different animal skins was necessary. It provided a visual imprint on a fabricated memory.

Another possible explanation for shapeshifting technology in the ancient world is the possibility of using frequency to alter perception. Chemical substances are not the only proven methods of influencing the brain. If ancient cultures were able to comprehend frequency deeply enough to develop medical and antigravitational applications, could they have also discovered how to use frequency to alter perception? Or can changing the frequency at which an object or biological entity vibrates actually change its physical composition? In which case, did ancient Earthlings really possess shapeshifting technology?

Was that knowledge obtained through self-learning, practice, and apprenticeship? Or did that knowledge come from the gods, aliens, time travelers, or the leftover survivors of a previous lost civilization of Earth?

Regardless of the origins, we have more mysteries about the technologies and knowledge of the ancient world than what mainstream scientists can provide acceptable explanations for or agree upon. The accounts provided in ancient text seem unrealistic to us because we use modern terms like technology, medicine, compound, and recipe to describe what people might have referred to as magic, elixir, potion, and spell. If we could meet our ancestors, view their methods, and show them ours how many parallels would we find?

Existence, awareness, reality, perception, the physical and the metaphysical all seem to be moving with, in, through, and around one another in an endless, simultaneous conjunction of cycles. The cycles for each move at their own pace. How long or short any one cycle can be is determined by a multitude of factors suggesting some cycles last longer than their predecessors and others shorter. With all that in mind it stands to reason that the invention, creation, loss, and reinvention of technologies as well as comprehension, imagination, and utilization of information would be no different. What if all the knowledge, ideas, and technologies we have now existed not only in our ancient history, but also in histories before ours? The forging of tools and mixing of compounds may be evolving and devolving in cycles as well. As life forms on this planet change, they gain, lose, and gain again.

Union of the Snake

One cycle that has long held the fascination of so many is the Astrological Cycle. Archeologists believe the astrological ages were important to many different cultures. Evidence suggests that the ancient cultures of Earth tracked every aspect of the night sky including the constellations and that they applied specific attributes and values to those constellations. Even today we are still checking our horoscopes and singing songs about specific astrological ages. Why did our ancestors place such significance on the various star formations? Why do we still concern ourselves with both our eastern and western Zodiac signs?

One reason could be that that we instinctually know the importance of the cosmic layout and the relationships between stars. Einstein's theory of Quantum Entanglement suggests that even if two molecules or objects are far apart, they can still potentially perceive and be affected by what happens to one another. Ernst Mach hypothesized that there is a relationship between the forces we can feel and observe here on Earth and those which exist elsewhere throughout the cosmos. If we delve a little deeper into both of these concepts and consider what we have thus far observed about forces, energies, and astral relationships, would we begin noticing correlations between an individual's Zodiac signs and specific measurable changes to both physical and metaphysical attributes of that individual during certain astrological alignments or events?

As a simple example, might we be able to observe the electromagnetic fields of individuals born under certain astrological conditions and compare them with others born under those exact conditions? Then might we observe how their EM fields react to different energies, changes in Earth's magnetic field, and specific astrological events? What if the constellations really do influence living organisms here on Earth as it rotates and orbits changing its location relative to the stars in those constellations?

Could it be as simple as cosmic movement produces subtle changes to the forces and energies on Earth influencing the formation of DNA as a living organism is conceived and/or developing? If the formation of an individual's DNA is determined by such influence, could our Zodiac signs really shape our personality? Did the ancient people of Earth notice correlations between personality types and the astrological conditions under which they occurred? Or were some people sensitive enough to perceive changes in magnetism or natural frequencies happening around them?

What if it is less about the physics and more about the math? Perhaps star formations simply provided recognizable patterns for which to base measurement systems. Could those patterns have also provided a convenient way for all creatures to communicate? It is thought that language began sometime around when the first humans started leaving cave art and drawing symbols. Earlier I questioned if we might be wrong about when ancient people developed language and written communication because we are unable to find or understand older methods. Could it be because the older method wasn't to write or draw, but to use the sky?

What if the constellations are the key to all ancient

knowledge, communications, and technologies? If they were used as a writing system similar to kanji or hieroglyphs, would we recognize it as written language? Perhaps we have merely been misinterpreting ancient clues all along. The ancient structures were often built to align with, map out, or in some way reference specific stars and constellations. Could the written history we're looking for be laid out for us in the form of megalithic star maps? Might each constellation have even had spoken sounds associated with them to form a spoken global and potentially universal language?

Almost all of the known ancient cultures seem to have the same gods and legends and while the names may vary, the constellations that represent them are the same across each culture. Could the constellations have been named after individuals who really did exist at one time? Was our prehistory recorded in the stars? Did survivors of previous resets use the stars to tell their stories to our ancestors?

So where does the snake fit into it all? The snake is also represented in all cultures but doesn't appear to have one clear constellation. There are several constellations having to do with the snake including the constellation of Draconis which curiously seems to correspond with Serpent Mound in Ohio. The two Babylonian serpent gods each have a constellation as well. There is also a year of the snake in the eastern zodiac, but exactly who does the snake represent?

Ancient cultures all over the world have documented constellations and often the same ones. Many seem to have some form of the Zodiac wheel. The Babylonians and Sumerians had a Zodiac wheel from which Ptolemy seemed to base his documentation of the constellations. The Greeks referred to the Zodiac wheel as the "language" of the gods. Could each Zodiac wheel of the ancient cultures have been the basis for, or in some way influenced their languages and writing? If so, might that explain why in so many cultures the snake is synonymous with wisdom?

To the Greeks the snake symbolized Aesculapius denoted in the sky by the constellation Ophiuchus and could be associated with Orion due to Aesculapius having used a snake to heal him. Ptolemy included the constellation of Serpens in the Almagest as the constellation representing the snake. However, the Chinese, though they recognize the snake as a zodiac, consider the Serpens constellation to be a representation of a wall. Chinses astrology dates back at least a thousand years before Ptolemy documented the Greek constellations, but the constellations are known to have also been important to the Mayans.

The cultures were as far apart from one another as they could be and yet they all knew of and depicted the constellations and included a snake mythos with a great deal of cultural significance. Was there an ancient global civilization that studied the constellations before the Mayans and Sumerians? Did this knowledge come from survivors of a previous reset? Could it have been brought to the ancient cultures of Earth from visiting extraterrestrials?

The Pleiades have also been considered a snake constellation in that they appear as a coiled snake and are occasionally considered to be the seven mothers of the world because they may have seeded the planet according to some legends. They are also associated with beauty, wisdom, and water, much like the snake. Interestingly enough the aboriginals of Australia believe they came from the Pleiades star system, and they believe their mother goddess is a rainbow serpent of creation and destruction. Another reason why the Pleiades is associated with the snake is that it's speculated that the Anunnaki may have come from a planet located in that system. This is due to there having been a depiction of seven stars that it presumed to be the Pleiades and the mention of seven Anunnaki.

The Hindu deity Shiva is also depicted with snakes and despite being commonly referred to as "he" has strikingly feminine features. Although Shiva is sometimes shown as half man and half woman, it is often said that the woman half is Parvati, Shiva's wife. However, many of the Hindi gods are able to shapeshift and change gender and are therefore sometimes considered to be androgenous. Shiva, whether male or female, is said to have wisdom, beauty, and power. Shiva wearing the snake also indicates a lack of fear and the ego that comes with being above others. Snakes in many cultures are associated with ego in some way often due to their representation of beauty and wisdom. In the Chinese Zodiac those born under the snake sign are said to be wise and beautiful, but also vain.

Also within the Hindi culture are amphibious snake hominids called Naga who can also change gender or be hermaphroditic. They supposedly built everything from below working their way up to the surface which indicates intelligence and skill. While not necessarily gods, the Naga are considered to be at least semidivine like demigods. Could the Naga have been one of our ancient hominid ancestors here on Earth? If so, were they an impressive culture of snake people respected and revered by other hominids? Might they have been the influence for the various snake legends throughout ancient cultures? Could they have even had wings or flight capability allowing them to visit newly emerging cultures all over the world as "flying serpent gods"? Perhaps they even inspired the Biblical Seraphim. We'll revisit the idea of the Naga having been the Seraphim a bit later, but for a moment let's indulge in a few less terrestrial possibilities.

With so many snake constellations to consider and so much emphasis on the snake in ancient mythologies one has to wonder where it all originated. Was there an ancient global snake culture here on Earth in prehistory which inspired other budding cultures? If so, did that culture have a star map of their own depicting a snake constellation we haven't considered? Or is it possible the snake actually represents Earth?

Assuming one of the afore mentioned snake constellations contain a planet from which our ancestors may have originated as some cultures and The Ancient Astronaut Theorists claim, could they have chosen Earth as their new home world because it was a habitable planet inside of what appeared to be a snake constellation from their perspective? The appearance of stars and their relationship to one another changes with each point of view. If we were to travel to another star system and gaze up at the sky towards Earth, would we see a constellation resembling a snake?

What if the snake isn't a constellation at all? The snake is often considered to be a creator or mother. The snake represents life, beauty, water, wisdom, freedom, woman, fertility, wrath, destruction, and a messenger of the gods in many different cultures. Could it be that the snake is the culmination or mother of all the constellations?

When one considers that the Zodiac actually has thirteen constellations due to the fact that the twelve signs all pass through Ophiuchus one could make the argument that Ophiuchus is the ruling constellation. Or one can make the argument that Earth is the single planet representing the mother snake ruling over the other constellations with them revolving around her. Not only are there thirteen constellations, but there are also thirteen crystal skulls. Could there be a crystal skull for each constellation including the snake? If so, what or who might the zodiacs really represent?

Perhaps before the last reset there were as many as twelve advanced nations each represented by a constellation and each in possession of a crystal skull with the thirteenth skull representing the combined nations under the mother constellation of the snake. If so, do the skulls act as suppositories for each nation with the thirteenth containing all the combined information?

A similar possibility is that Earth functioned as a neutral planet in a young solar system for ancient interstellar diplomats from planets located in each of the constellations to converge and discuss interplanetary politics. If Earth is a neutral planet in a relatively young star system and life has been spreading through the cosmos encountering other life and occasionally warring with other life, could Earth be a safe haven for refugees from twelve extraterrestrial societies who may have formed a treaty with one another? If so, maybe Homo Sapien isn't the only invasive nonnative Earth species, just the most potent one.

Perhaps the constellations aren't meant to represent where we came from, but where some of us have gone. What if at one time there was an advance global language derived from Astrology that the various advance nations of Earth used to communicate with one another? Perhaps this is also how they shared their knowledge in other disciplines such as math and chemistry. If so, could the individual nations have been represented by different constellations? If the last reset was caused by an ancient war, could each nation have chosen to send evacuees to their corresponding constellations in search of habitable planets? Might they have already known of specific planets in each constellation capable of sustaining life? If each nation did send refugees to planets in their constellations, was this a predetermined plan in case of global war? Had the nations agreed that in the event of a natural calamity, global unrest, or unresolvable differences between one another each nation would depart from Earth for separate planets?

If previous inhabitants of Earth did colonize other planets, could they have left behind information pertaining to their destination for descendants or newly emerging cultures to eventually follow? For example, what if their various cultures claiming to be from the Pleiades or Orion systems don't have ancestors who came from those locations, but who instead went to those locations? If so, why were they left behind? Was there a lottery?

If the constellations were used as an ancient global language and different cultures were represented by specific constellations maybe that's all there was to it. Could it simply be that some of that knowledge survived and inspired the current constellation system we have today? It's possible that our ancestors knew the importance of star formations, but enough knowledge was lost to cause significant changes in the established star maps. What if the constellations identified by the Mayan, Egyptians, Chinese, and Greeks were not the same constellations as previous lost cultures? What stars might ancient Earthlings have been able to see that we can no longer see today? Could there have been a snake constellation of the ancient world which greatly influenced life on Earth?

If the snake is the mother constellation and represents creation and life, could various spiral symbols and coiled snakes found in ancient cultures be intended to preserve that knowledge? Might this not only be an attempt by our ancestors to show us Earth as an egg nestled in a coiled snake but also being protected and nurtured by the constellations? Is there a greater cosmic meaning behind this? Could this represent the formation of solar systems, galaxies, or even the entire cosmos?

Or could the snake simply represent who we are as inhabitants of Earth? Perhaps the original evolved Earthling were amphibious or reptilian. There were beings described in several ancient mythologies as having been here prior to our creation or arrival. Even the Bible has left openings for interpretation and while it later mentions several different peoples, their origins are often unknown or unspecified. There is even a vague description of Syrophoenicians which the Bible only describes as "perhaps a mixed race of Syrians and Phoenicians". The fact that the word "perhaps" is used indicates to me that there are even people in the Bible whose lineage cannot be accounted for. What if the Syrophoenicians were not a mix race of Syrians and Phoenicians, but instead a mix race of Seraphim and Phoenicians? As for the Seraphim, they are described as being "an order of celestial beings" which leaves a great deal of room for interpretation and speculation.

For instance, what exactly does it mean to be "an order of celestial beings"? Many people consider celestial beings to mean angels, of which there seem to be different types and different ranks in the Bible. Ancient Astronaut Theorists consider celestial beings to mean extraterrestrials. What if the Seraphim were a previous race of Earthlings? Perhaps they were only talked about by survivors of other ancient races and romanticized into legend by newly emerging cultures like the Israelites and Egyptians. What if "an order of celestial beings" means a group of people or a nation represented by a constellation? Could celestial orders have referred to various ancient cultures or even races?

What if the reason we only know of four is because they were the only ones to have survived the last reset? Could there have been remnants of four ancient celestial orders who shared knowledge with newly emerging humans and inspired legends? Or could there have been more than four, but only certain beings were considered to belong to a celestial order or only four of them were willing to interact with newly emerging humans? What if the Seraphim represent an ancient amphibious or reptilian race? Could they have been the oldest and most advanced surviving Earth race? Or at least one of the oldest and most advanced?

What if the Seraphim are the beings also described as Kapa, Mermaids, and/or Naga? Could they have influenced cultures all over the world? What if they are the very beings who rebuilt civilizations after the last reset? Might that explain the various ancient cultures of the Americas having a flaming, plumed, and/or flying serpent for a god? Or the aboriginal Australians having the Rainbow Serpent, the Hindi having Naga, the Japanese having Kapa, and the Dogon having Nommo? Might it also explain why the snake represents life, water, creation, and wisdom?

If the Seraphim were an ancient snake-like hominid here on Earth, where did they go? Did they eventually die out or interbreed with our ancestors until we could discern no visible trace? Did they leave the planet? Are they hiding in caves or in the ocean? What if they actually evolved in the ocean? If all sorts of different hominids did evolve in a plethora of environments at various times here on Earth could there have been at least one amphibious hominid? What if one of our ancestors did evolve deep in the ocean and eventually evolved to be able to live on land, but not in the sun? Could that ancestor have then evolved to live in caves until eventually either slowly adapting to sunlight or interbreeding with another ancestor to produce a viable hybrid able to withstand the sun? Is it possible that portions of both cave dwelling and ocean dwelling ancestors still exist in deep places we are yet unable to reach?

Before I asked if life might have evolved underground, deep in caves, or in oceans and slowly migrated towards the surface. This may be one explanation for the Naga race and why they built by carving outward from within the Earth. Another explanation is that some life forms, including some dinosaurs, managed to escape the big dinosaur extinction by fleeing into caverns and adapting to life underground. If some dinosaurs survived that event and evolved into birds, could others have evolved into intelligent reptilian hominids?

Assuming for a moment that there was an advanced global snake race, Seraphim or otherwise, and that race was the original Earth race, can all other Earth hominids be traced back to that potentially amphibious race? What if that's why there seem to be evolutionary gaps? If our oldest hominid ancestor evolved in the ocean and then later amphibious branches emerged could the evidence be at the bottom of our deepest oceans, lakes, and submerged caves? Could some of our ancestors have been completely eradicated along with any evidence of their existence due to the events of previous resets? Perhaps we will only ever be able to find our more recent ancestors. Could the remains of their missing predecessors be forever lost to time?

However, if the snake hominid is the original ancestor to all other Earth hominids, could it have also managed to survive well into the emergence of Homo Sapiens? If Homo Sapians are an invasive species did our DNA come from a hominid that didn't evolve on Earth? If so, did our DNA just happen to fall here or was that ancestral hominid advanced enough to travel here? If another advanced race did come here and find Earth already occupied by an equally advance snake race, did they go to war with one another? Were our snake ancestors conquered and vilified by an ancestor who did come from a planet in the Pleiades or Orion?

Some individuals have a stronger connection to Earth and to specific astronomical events than others. Could it be that those people are more sensitive to magnetic fields and subtle changes to them? Does that make them more equipped for life on this planet? Are they better able to sense environmental changes? Can they communicate with others, including animals, by relaying feelings and intentions instinctually and without conscious recognition? Perhaps such individuals are more closely related to the hominids that evolved here on Earth than to whatever ancestor or ancestors that may have come from elsewhere.

Could modern humans possessing certain genes or more genes from an ancient snake ancestor have a stronger connection to the planet? Could those ancient genes be responsible for certain other desirable attributes such as heightened perception, higher intelligence, or even physical traits associated with beauty? Could stronger ancestry to the snake result in anomalous people? For example, what if what some Native American tribes call "star children" actually have stronger ties to Earth? What if it's a strong connection to the planet that enables a strong connection to the cosmos? Could ancient genomes have a stronger natural connection than more recent genomes? Or if there are human ancestors not native to this planet, could those who evolved on Earth have simply been more in tune with this location in the cosmos while those who traveled here somehow lost their natural connection? Are individuals possessing stronger instincts and sensitivities to the natural world tapping into latent DNA of an ancient ancestor? Or are these individuals the evolutionary culmination of all our ancient ancestors?

Many people consider those who possess extra sensory abilities to be more highly evolved and those beings are also often more intelligent. However, it's said that when a species reaches an evolutionary plateau reproduction stalls. There seems to be a pattern of geniuses and other gifted individuals not producing offspring. Often this is attributed to their focus or even obsession with their life passions or their social awkwardness, but what if these individuals have simply reached the evolutionary plateau of the human species?

Going back to the possibility of an interplanetary alignment between twelve planets, if such a war broke out from one planet invading another would the rest of the planets get involved? Could there have been an attack made against Earth by an alliance of planets? If Earth was representing by the snake and the snake needed to be conquered, why? Did the snake become too powerful? Did the snake's representation of freedom somehow undermine authority? What if another planet, or even another race here on Earth, set out to conquer all the others? Perhaps the snake rose up to defend freedom and protect life? Could that be why the snake has such reverence in so many cultures?

We have seen how power, idealism, and mass genocide of those who don't agree or are deemed less worthy has shaped our known history. What if such dark ages are also cyclical and have occurred in civilizations prior to the last reset? Could there have been a Hitler type figure or a Vatican like organization which actually succeeded in his or her or their endeavors? If there existed a previous global snake culture on Earth founded in knowledge and freedom perhaps this threatened the ideas of another, more restrictive culture. Could there have been an authoritative society which condemned freedom and exploration?

In our own history we have seen Christianity emerge and condemn all other religions destroying the vast multicultural civilizations of the ancient world, Hitler come into power and declared the Arian race to be the superior race and seek to eliminate others, and the Vatican declared science and many of the ancient practices to be heresy launching humanity into dark ages. These are just a few examples of how one person or one organization gaining power can obliterate the previous state of the world. All it takes is one intent rooted in a notion, a belief, a fear, or a desire to spark conflict and potentially lead to devastating consequences. Could an individual or nation in Earth's distant past have opposed the concepts of the snake and initiated a great conflict?

What if there was a powerful nation which sought to enslave another or create artificial slaves? If the snake represents freedom, could one civilization enacting a slave policy have started to a world war? Or if new hominids were emerging to look less like their reptilian or amphibious ancestors, could they have grown disgusted with or fearful of those who resembled snakes? Might that have led to a snake genocide? Could some of this knowledge have survived the ancient past and been preserved in the beginnings of our history? Could it have been altered by misunderstandings, differing interpretations, and inaccurate translations? If the culture that challenged that of the snake emerged victorious could the accounts have been intentionally altered?

Were survivors of the snake culture banished to remote parts of the planet? Did they retreat underground? Could they have fled into space? Might they have been imprisoned or enslaved? There is an Ancient Egyptian hieroglyph that some have speculated to be a lotus or possibly a lightbulb, but appears to me to be a snake imprisoned, and possibly being tortured, within something. The Ancient Egyptians did have stories of the snake god Apophis being conquered and tortured. Could this just be a coincidence?

If the snake also represents beauty, mother, and fertility could the snake culture have been a matriarchal society? If so, could the fall of the snake have been due to the rise of men? Could one or more Patriarchal society or societies have emerged in opposition to the snake, and potentially other Matriarchal societies, and set out to establish a world in which women were no longer permitted to have power? Might this be the reason for women often representing fire, rage, wrath, villains, and sin? Could this also be the source of stories about goddesses like Lilith, Maftet, Pele, Pyrrha, Pandora, Kali, and the Amazons?

If an ancient battle of the sexes really did occur, what was the reason? Were women mistreating the men under their control? Were they mistrustful of men and so would not allow them to hold positions of power or be an intricate part of society? Were men resentful of women because the women ruled over society while the men were made to tend to the heavy labor or sent off to war? Or was it more primal and need driven? Did the men merely get fed up with not being allowed to have their way with women? Did arrogance play a role? Could women have thought themselves more intelligent and therefore superior? Could men have thought themselves stronger and therefore superior?

Whoever this mysterious snake society may have been and whatever the reason for their apparent collapse, could the various serpent mounds found all over the planet have been left as proof they were here? Were these mounds just prominent decorations of a global serpentine society or did they serve a purpose? If the survivors of the snake people were viewed as gods, could they have been created by later cultures in worship of them? Do these mounds have any relation to the constellations? If so, could they have been left as warnings or some other kind of message?

What if the snake society of Earth was the ancient civilization responsible for all the megalithic creations and ancient knowledge before being lost to a natural, unpreventable cataclysmic event? If that event was something astrological, like a meteor strike, were they able to predict it in time to escape to the heavens and leave behind a warning for future inhabitants?

Could the lost knowledge concerning the importance of the astrological ages reveal pertinent information about Earth's cycles? For example, if the Earths pole do suddenly change approximately every 25,000 to 26,000 years causing drastic global environmental changes, could this coincide with the approximate 25,772 years it takes to cycle through all twelve astrological ages?

If so, might the ancient cultures of Earth have understood this correlation and tracked the astrological ages in order to escape the devastation? If we could uncover that lost knowledge, could we predict the next reset in time to also escape into the heavens? Might we find survivors of Earth ancient civilizations, possibly even those of the snake, once we reach the technological understanding required to travel to distant planets?

Darwin May Be Half Right

The problem with Darwin's Theory of Evolution is that it's over a century and a half old and scientists are still trying to fill in the holes by looking for "missing links". What if there are none? What if we can't follow a linear species to species evolution because it's far more complicated than natural selection?

It's likely Darwin was right about certain species having evolved from others and splitting off into different branches, but what if it didn't happen gradually? Many believe it is possible for sudden leaps in evolution to occur due to singular events or other external influences. For example, if an expecting mother becomes infected with a virus that dramatically alters the DNA of her unborn child, that child might be born an entirely new species. Now say that this virus spread across the entire population and all the expecting mothers gave birth to this new offspring. Suddenly a new species emerged from its predecessor at once from a single event.

Many living organisms probably do share some ancestry with one another in their distant family trees, but as I asked earlier, could so much thriving life have really come from one common primordial ancestor? Also, could missing ancestors really just be the result of "survival of the fittest" in which they were unable to adapt and so died off? Is the reason we can't verify links in evolution through the fossil record really due to extinction events? Or is Darwin's theory merely one small piece to a far more complex puzzle?

Perhaps all the theories are each a piece to our ancestral puzzle. We know that the building blocks of life can be found all around. As mentioned earlier, genetic information can even exist in the harshness of space in viruses and even in some microorganisms. So why do we still treat Darwin's theory as a single event? Why do we view it as the big bang of life on earth, instead of one piece to an intricate ongoing process?

Perhaps we should be looking at all the various theories of evolution along with other origin theories as a whole. Could Darwin have been right about some species simply dying off due to an inability to adapt to their changing environments? Could they have simply changed with their environments to become something else entirely? If they did change into something else, would their DNA differ so drastically from the species they once were that we are unable to make the genetic connection?

As various forms of life encountered one another genetic information was exchanged, mutations and adaptations occurred, and new genetic material was created. Eventually larger life forms emerged that were similar enough to one another to produce viable offspring. Environments influenced evolution and likely did cause the extinction of organisms who were unable to adapt and the evolution of others. Although life may have developed in one location thousands of years after life in another, and potentially even on other planets before somehow finding its way here, if the environmental conditions and genetic information were similar enough, the organisms that developed may have eventually merged into one through generations of interbreeding. Therefore, the two proceeding species may appear to be related to one another, but entirely unrelated to the current. When in actuality the two proceeding species would have been unrelated to each other, while both being ancestors to the current.

This may be exactly how modern humans came about over time and might explain why there seem to have been several different types of ancient humans which has since bottle-necked into one. What if many were never really the same species but were still close enough to interbreed? Evidence has been found that early homo sapiens did intermingle and produce offspring with Neanderthals. Perhaps even the various 'races' of humans that we see today each have a different ancestor. We may have all been different species who eventually became different races of one species through coexisting and creating offspring with one another. This would explain our diverse genetics and possibly even our evolutionary leaps.

If different species of hominids evolved from separate evolutionary trees down parallel paths, we may have evolved into the beings we are today not from survival of the fittest, but from coexisting and collaboration of the eventual merging of the various species. There may have even been dozens of humanoid life forms roaming the planet at one time all cooperating and benefiting from the diversifying of genetic information.

With all the other the previously mentioned theories of how humans came to be on this planet is it time to retire Darwin's theory of evolution? After over a hundred and fifty years perhaps we should at least expand upon it and incorporate it into a larger collection of human history as one potential chapter of many.

Ancient Astronaut Theorists May Be Half Right

Ancient Astronaut Theorists may also be half right. There's no reason to assume life is unique to Earth and human-like beings are only found on Earth. "Humans" by majority accepted definition may be unique to this planet, but this planet is not unique. Life on other Earthlike planets may not only look like us, but they may contain nearly identical DNA. In fact, their DNA may be close enough to ours to produce fertile offspring capable of reproducing with one another, other Earthlings, and other Extraterrestrials which would classify them and us as the same species.

Even most mainstream scientists can agree the probability of life elsewhere is high. For most, the argument isn't whether or not there is life on other planets, but whether or not that life is intelligent, capable of interstellar and/or intergalactic travel, and if their method of such travel can cover the distance between our two worlds. Could there be human-like beings capable of such travel making frequent visits to other star systems and even other galaxies, but only within a certain proximity? If they happen to be millions or billions of light years away from the Milky Way galaxy, we may be just outside of what they might consider reasonable time and distance.

Some scientists drop off early on in the debate believing the only other life in our universe to be microbial. Others agree intelligent life forms, and maybe even other intelligent bipedal beings, do exist, but are too far away to reach or even communicate with us. Still, some argue that regardless of whether or not life elsewhere is microbial or complex, it may not be capable of surviving Earth's atmosphere. Even if life evolved on a planet similar to Earth and travel here, too much or too little of any one element can have detrimental effects to organisms not intended for our planet's conditions.

What if life forms on other Earth-like planets are not carbon based? Some scientists have proposed the possibility of Silicon, Sulfur, Ammonia, Phosphorous and Germanium being potential base elements of life in the right conditions. Could Earth sustain such life forms if they were to arrive here? Could there be life forms based on other elements we haven't even considered like Calcium? If so, might some of those life forms be able to survive on Earth? Might certain life form be able to adapt and eventually evolve into new carbon-based generations? Much of our assumptions about which elements we could potentially see as "life-based" elements are based off what we know about amino acids, DNA, and RNA. However, could there be life forms on other planets derived from a slightly different blueprint?

If we are going to split hairs about it, we should also consider the other aspects of The Ancient Astronaut Theory. One such being that our potential alien ancestors did not have to be hominids. That aspect argues that humanity could have evolved from amino acids, viruses, or even microbial life such as something like a tardigrade which have been proven resilient enough to withstand prolonged exposure to space. How did they get here from space? They could have hitched a ride on a comet or even off a long-distance probe from another world.

The Ancient Astronaut Theory doesn't limit our alien

forerunners to arriving by high tech space craft. Many agree that a more likely scenario in that life did hitch a ride on something. Panspermia, the seeding of our planet by microbial life, is widely accepted as a reasonable argument for alien ancestry. The opposing views of Panspermia being was it directed by intelligent design or was it was merely accidental happenstance?

Regardless of which part or parts of the theory we apply to our potential history we can't answer all the questions and it doesn't exclude any of the other creation theories. We can, however, incorporate all of the other theories seamlessly into the Ancient Astronaut Theory. If we only choose to accept Panspermia, we can still satisfy the religious notion that God or the gods created us by orchestrating and directing the seeding of the planet. Then, as Darwin suggested, some life died out while some life adapted and evolved. However, as my Agar Plate Theory proposes, that doesn't mean all life evolved from the same location on earth, at the same rate, or from the same microbial. Some life may have advanced, created civilizations, and left behind mysteries for the new life to ponder before vanishing to a global extinction event, being consumed by newly evolved life, or left the planet only for the cycle to repeat.

Our solar system is relatively young compared to others. Perhaps life has been spreading from planet to planet, solar system to solar system, galaxy to galaxy and so on from the start. Life may travel across great expanses in a dormant state within asteroids, comets, and various space debris only to fall to a newly formed planet and evolve based on that planet's conditions. Once it becomes capable of space exploration, life may then depart in search of new planets to propagate. Or if a planet is destroyed before life can evolve to that point, potential remnants of life may be preserved in the remaining fragments of the planet only to repeat the cycle. Thus, life could be in a perpetual state of planet hopping. Could it be that older galaxies are dying, or even already dead, and life has persisted from those galaxies to Earth over millennia?

That's just one possible melding of the various theories into a single cohesive timeline. It's also possible that other beings did visit, crash land, and/or settle on our planet sometime in our past adding diversity to our gene pool. According to many different ancient cultures, beings did come here from the heavens. Some even specify the solar system from which those beings came. Perhaps this explains why all modern humans are Homo Sapien.

If Homo Sapien is an invasive species not native to this planet, it may be that the many hominids of Earth bottlenecking down to one was the unintended result of a foreign species breeding with various natives. If the entity responsible crashed or became stranded here, interbreeding was inevitable. Some have speculated that Mars may have once been inhabited and that survivors of a Martian cataclysm came to Earth. If that's true, Homo Sapien may be the hominid species native to Mars who came here as refugees.

However, if an entity was just passing through or was a recurring visitor there may have been some recklessness or even malice involved depending on the entity's intent. If Earth has had regular visits from other beings, is it possible those visits have continued without our notice?

If there are entities, biological or robotic, making frequent visits to this planet there are any number of reasons for why we can't see them, touch them, or communicate with them. Most of these reasons would also render the sharing of genetic information impossible.

If the entities responsible for UFO sightings and crashes are nothing more than self-sustaining remote-control drones or robots acting as probes for another planet, they may not contain anything biological, or if they did, it may not be compatible with us or our atmosphere. If there are phase shifting, inter-dimensional, or ethereal entities they may only be able to alter our perception and nothing more.

If there are superior beings watching over our planet for any reason, there is a distinct possibility they don't want anything to do with humanity. Throughout our history we haven't been the most hospitable race, even towards one another. From a visitor's perspective the planet may be a welcoming site, but the inhabitants are strong deterrents.

By that reasoning maybe we are being visited and studied. If intelligent beings have been studying us for millennia, they may only be passive observers and have had no interactions with us or any of Earth's previous inhabitants. They may have watched a seemingly hopeless race reset itself via our violent nature, technologies beyond our control, or any number of catastrophes each time thinking to themselves 'maybe this time'. Maybe they continue watching out of bewilderment, maybe curiosity, or maybe they really are hoping that one of these eons Earth will see a cycle in which the inhabitants reach an acceptable degree of evolution to interact with our extraterrestrial voyeurs.

There are so many possibilities to this theory any or none of which could be part of Earth's unknown history. Even if it's not part of our past it could be part of our future. Even if biological information from extraterrestrial sources hasn't made it to our planet yet, some day we, or our probes, may find genetic information on other planets and incorporate it into life on this planet, maybe even ourselves.

Roswell, New Mexico

When discussing the possibility of other worldly visitors and crashed ships it's difficult to avoid the specific 1947 incident of Roswell, New Mexico. This is one of the most infamous and well debated subjects related to extraterrestrials, conspiracy theories, government cover-up, and media frenzies. Mention to someone or research any one of these topics and the question of what really happened at Roswell is bound to be included.

Well, this is a collection of theories and my own speculation so I wouldn't be doing my due diligence if this were left out, and I have my own thoughts on this one too. Although to most a familiar subject, it's probably fair to say there isn't much in the way of verified facts or even evidence. Instead, we have an abundance of speculation and misinformation.

Let's start with what most would agree. Something happened. There are some who would disagree to even that. The people of Roswell were startled by something falling out of the sky with at least some velocity visibly impacting the ground and leaving debris. Vague explanations out of the way, the item was initially unidentified, had presumably been flying prior to falling, and was an object. Therefore, it did, and still does, meet the nomenclature criteria for Unidentified Flying Object.

The people of Roswell had seen, heard, and then found the impact. The United States Military arrived on scene to inspect and collect evidence from the site. The initial press reports headlined that the U.S. Army re-covered a flying disc on a ranch just outside of Roswell. The press later released that it was a weather balloon. A later story released by the U.S. government was that in was in fact a weather balloon, but it was an experimental nuclear weather balloon and therefore required discretion.

Regardless of whether it was a disc or a balloon, no explanation provided by the U.S. Government on this subject matter has ever helped their case. The people were unable to believe what they had been told by their government which only lead to more distrust and speculation.

In the years since 1947 other reports concerning the crash have come to light, but they have only created more confusion. There have also been many claims of evidence and whistle blowers emerging. In a case such as this with too much publicity, confusion, misinformation, unverifiable claims, contradicting reports, and years since the event occurred allowing hype to become legend, any credible evidence or accounts get lost in the fray.

To say an Unidentified Flying Object crashed in Roswell isn't untrue, but as to whether or not the object was later identified and accurately disclosed to the press without any cover-up, we can only guess. We all have our own theories based on the bits we believe and the bits we don't. There are so many that even just trying to summarize them all would be daunting.

Therefore, I will share what I believe happened without naming or laying claim to this theory because I'm aware that I may not be the only person to have considered this scenario. Unfortunately, I can't be as light-hearted in my explanation of what I suspect may have happened as I was with my general summary of the Roswell hype. Suppose the crash and the cover-up were both due to darker events still recent enough in hearts across the world that any reminders would just reopen wounds.

The Roswell crash happened in 1947 only two years after World War Two ended. Countries were still re-building, recovering, and reconciling. Some skirmishes were still occurring. Families were still grieving and fearful. Soldiers were still missing. Some soldiers re-mained unaware that the war was over until they were found and brought home years later. Some soldiers wouldn't be found and informed the war had ended un-til decades later.

What if Kamikaze pilots, unaware of Japan's sur-render, continued to attempt dive-bombs on U.S. bases? The Roswell crash was just five miles north of Walker Air Force Base which was active during the second world war. Keep in mind that this was the Air Force Base where experimental technologies were being developed and from where the nuclear bombs were de-ployed. Considering the damage done to Hiroshima and Nagasaki, it is entirely possible that some Japanese pi-lots were angry enough to target the base even after the treaty had been signed. Could Japanese pilots have been launching attacks towards U.S. bases?

Kamikaze pilots most often target enemy ships around their islands, but they were involved with attack on Pearl Harbor and as such were capable of getting their planes over greater distances if they thought they had reason to. There are smaller, isolated islands between our west coast and the Hawaii islands where they may have fled or regrouped. Any pilots on those islands likely wouldn't have known the war had ended.

Just one month before Roswell there were incidents involving UFOs and "fallen debris" over Maury Island which was also located on the west coast not too far from a U.S. Air Force Base. Could Japanese pilots stranded on isolated islands after the Pearl Harbor attack, with no way of knowing the war had ended, and likely not enough jet fuel to get them out of enemy territory, have conceived a way to get at least a handful of planes over U.S. airspace?

Prior to the reported Maury Island incident there was the infamous Battle for Los Angeles in February 1942. This is most often referred to as a false alarm that occurred due to heightened emotions and panic after the December 1941 attack on Pearl Harbor. There does, however, remain the question of what might've been seen in the skies over Los Angeles. Only two days before the Battle of L.A. a Japanese submarine had surfaced off the coast of Santa Barbara and attacked an oil field. This certainly increased concern over potential enemy attacks enough to cause false alarms, but is that all it really was?

Some have suggested the sighting that triggered the Battle of Los Angeles may have been extraterrestrial in nature. Others attribute it to wartime jitters and inexperienced military personal mistakenly reacting to something mundane. Still others insist that it really was an attack from Japanese aircraft. What if this incident really was triggered by a UFO belonging not to an extraterrestrial source, but to the Japanese?

Did they possess a superior technology? Has the information concerning such technology been kept secret all this time? Is it possible the U.S. government didn't want the already panicked populace learning that Japan had a technological advantage and were capable of reaching the west coast? During those tumultuous times the government did take extra care to avoid inciting panic among the American people. Could the reason for continued secrecy after the war be due to an agreement between the two governments to stifle public concerns and share technology?

If the Battle of Los Angeles was an attack by Japanese aircraft, could the Maury Island incident have also been an attempted attack? Was it intercepted and prevented by the U.S. and swept under the rug to prevent public fear and international ramifications? Why did it take six years after the Pearl Harbor attack? Why did they miss their marks? Did they even have the fuel to attempt an attack? Why would the U.S. government conceal attempted enemy attacks on Air Force bases?

There are many reasons why it might have taken them six years after their attack on Pearl Harbor. Their planes may have been hit or had mechanical issues causing crash landings in the oceans. A pilot shot down into the ocean would have likely been disoriented at the least. They could have been near enough to a small island when they went down or been towed to an island by submarine.

Once stranded, they would have gotten their bearings, tended their wounds, and assessed their situation. Their planes were probably damaged and low on fuel and if they were towed by a submarine, it was likely in too rough of a condition to attempt to make it out of enemy waters. Multiple planes, pilots, and possibly a submarine would have provided parts and people for repairs and it's not unreasonable that they could have salvaged enough fuel for three or more planes.

As for missing their marks, if those Air Force Bases were their targets, they weren't off by much and that's after potentially being stranded, possibly injured, on an isolated island in unfamiliar territory with limited equipment and resources. Or if the attacks didn't come from a leftover pilot, they could have been unsanctioned

171

attacks from rogue loyalists of General Tojo.

If the Roswell crash was that of a Kamikaze the U.S. military would have known immediately, especially after the first two attempts a month prior over Maury Island. The military would have been obligated to contain and silence the incidents in order to avoid inciting public panic or straining international cooperation. Japan had surrendered and signed a treaty, the U.S. was establishing bases and relations, and enough residual grief and anger lingered throughout the world to potentially start the war anew if countries attacked one another again.

If the Roswell incident was truly an unfortunate post war circumstance the U.S. Government had every reason and right to cover that up. They may have recovered a small, unrecognizable body and a bizarre disc shaped aircraft. After six years struggling to survive on an island with the likelihood of prolonged dehydration, malnourishment, and exposure combined with injuries that healed wrong only to crash a plane into a desert, anyone's body would appear alien. Bodies can also appear smaller and misshapen after burning which may contribute to any "alien" appearance.

The planes appearance can be explained by pilots piecing parts together and making alterations to lighten it enough to stretch out the fuel or by Japan simply having unusual and undocumented crafts. Initial personal arriving on scene may not have been properly briefed to know what to expect and may have embarrassingly jumped to conclusions resulting in impulsive comments contradictory to the statements given by senior military personal later.

There's also the possibility that the U.S. military and government wasn't aware that the aircraft or crafts and body or bodies recovered at Roswell were Japanese until later examination. If at the time of recovery, the appearance of any craft or body couldn't immediately be identified as human the military may have suspected something other worldly. In which case, could they have been fully prepared to disclose an alien crash to the people? Was the military initially excited by the prospect of finding an intelligent life form from another planet and therefore jumped the gun when first speaking to the press? If the crash had turned out to be aliens and flying saucers and not Japanese Kamikaze would the government have been more forthcoming?

If the Roswell crash was an attempted Kamikaze attack and the U.S. military did recover the plane and body, the plane may have been kept for further study and the body secretly returned to Japan. Both the U.S. and Japanese governments may still be keeping such an incident secret. In my opinion government secrecy would be excused under these circumstances. This was just one more theory to consider adding to the many already out there concerning the 1947 crash in Roswell, New Mexico. However, there are yet more possibilities to consider.

Along the same line of thought, not all Nazi soldiers were accounted for after the war and mysteries still surround the supposed technologies they may have had. Could they have had an experimental craft or crafts with which to attack the U.S.? If so, why wait until 1947? Were the crafts not yet ready? Was the lapse in time due to difficulties they faced in hiding? Perhaps we weren't attacked at all.

What if it was one of our own experimental craft that crashed? It could be as simple as the Army having gotten to the site before the Air Force. The different military branches have their own top-secret endeavors and don't always share information with one another. It could be that the Air Force was working on a craft which appeared alien to the Army upon their arrival. It was the Army who gave the initial statement that they had found a crashed disc. Perhaps it was the Air Force who then instructed personal at the scene to alter their statement in the interest of national security.

However, sometimes a weather balloon really is just a weather balloon. With experimental nuclear technologies being developed by the Air Force and a massive electrical storm being reported in the area it could have been a new top-secret nuclear weather balloon sent out to gather data on the storm. The government did issue a statement that, yes, the Roswell incident was a cover-up, but not of an extraterrestrial craft. In the official U.S. report, the government claims that is was a weather balloon, but it was an experimental nuclear balloon. Of course, there are many who still don't buy this explanation either.

Assuming for a moment that the craft did come from beings more advanced than ourselves, might those beings have still been terrestrial? Instead of aliens from space, could some hidden ancient ancestors have been responsible for the incident at Roswell? If there were and still are advanced amphibious beings, such as Naga, hiding in the waters of Earth our development and use of nuclear technology might be a concern to them. We share the planet. It's reasonable to assume that if there is a clandestine superior race of beings monitoring and interfering with our nuclear technologies it is because they don't want us causing further harm to their planet.

Another possible explanation for Roswell and for UFOs in general would be the bending of light and or space to allow us to occasionally see objects from a different time and for those objects to pass from their time into ours under specific conditions. Theoretically it is possible to bend space such that we might view or even travel through time. There are also anomalies in space and time which we still do not fully understand. Could the gravitational and/or electromagnetic field of Earth have experienced a change as to cause an overlap in time such that the present and future were to occur simultaneously?

What if the UFOs we see are actually our own future craft? Could these be intentional visits by time travelers? Could the UFOs that crash in our time be from accidents our future selves are making in an effort to perfect time travel? Or could they even be the past craft of ancient civilizations before us? If flying saucers were recovered at Roswell, could they have been the result of another timeline briefly crossing into ours? If so, did they come from our future or from our past? What if these were the Vimana of Ancient India? Could they have been experimenting with time travel in order to leave a time period of Earth experiencing a reset? Were they fleeing the Brahmastra that was said to have been capable of destroying the world? Or were they simply caught unexpectedly in a space-time anomaly? Some experts believe energy vortexes have the potential to act as wormholes connecting to points of space and/or time. They also believe that these vortexes appear randomly and often in places of higher electromagnetic readings.

The possibilities are endless when we consider that what we are seeing may be the result of cosmic forces interacting with one another in ways we are only just beginning to explore. If changes in space time here on Earth allow us to see craft from the past or the future, could there be situations in which those craft are able to pass into our time from theirs? Or might these events happen at random? Could wormholes be opening up and swallowing aircraft, animals, and even people and depositing them into another time? If so, might we be witnessing aircraft from the future as UFOs and Plesiosaurus from the past as mysterious lake monsters? Could this explain some seemingly impossible sightings and encounters of the world? Could it also explain vanishings, including mass disappearances of entire civilizations, and sudden arrivals of different beings throughout history?

If the Roswell crash was the result of overlapping timelines, would the U.S. military have mistaken it for an extraterrestrial event? Would they have been able to determine if an event was extraterrestrial or interdimensional at that time? If at any point the U.S. government did discover that the Roswell crash was the result of a space-time anomaly, would there be a need for secrecy? Could there be scientists studying the incident for potential insight into time travel applications or other top secret scientific endeavors?

Are such events trackable? Did ancient cultures know how to predict when a time rift would occur at specific locations? If so, could they have used the knowledge to intentionally travel through the rift? If these events are trackable and certain ancestors did figure out how to predict a rift, did they leave the information behind for us to decipher? Is that why some ancient cultures left petroglyphs reported to be of portals? Have our scientists already figured this out? Could this be part of whatever secret government project there may be on the matter?

Considering this theory as a possibility, could it also explain how scientists have since been able to create the technologies to propel us into space? Did we gain knowledge and technology from another time? Or could we have already been experimenting with clandestine technologies at Walker Air Force Base and the entire Roswell case was just the result of a military experiment gone awry? It seems Roswell may forever remain a mystery and therefore fertile topic of theory crafters from all disciplines.

MIB

Another popular topic of debate when considering government denial and stifling information is what and who are the Men In Black aka the MIB. Before we ask what are they, who are they, and what is their mission, we first need to ask do they even exist? The reported UFO sightings of Maury Island are often credited for the MIB's unsavory reputation.

The 1947 Maury Island UFO incidents, which preceded the Roswell crash by only a month, was reported by two men who claimed pieces of metal fell from a craft braking a man's arm and killing a dog. They then contacted an Air Force officer to report that strange men in black suits attempted to intimidate them into silence about the incident.

This resulted in an investigation by officers of the U.S. Air Force who determined the metal fragments presented to them as evidence to be inconsequential. However, the Air Force Officers died in a crash on their way back from the investigation which only prompted more suspicion. The FBI was called in to investigate the crash and deaths of the Air Force officers.

The reported 'men in black' could have been the FBI or the Air Force officers if the Air Force officers were wearing dark blue uniforms which could have been mistaken for men in black suits. There wasn't much physical evidence to support the claims, but other people did claim to have seen strange craft or crafts flying over and there were other reported UFO sightings in the area.

Could sightings of aircraft that appear to locals as unusual could have been due to U.S. Air Force craft coming and going?

Did U.S. aircraft flying overhead inspire the story? Did uniformed Air Force officers investigating, then advising against sharing their story, even if it was only meant as a friendly warning against nothing more than potential ridicule and embarrassment, instigate further exaggerations from the claimants? Another possible scenario is that the reported sighting was made in earnest after something did happen which alarmed the men enough to genuinely believe their own claims.

Presuming the previously provided alternative theory for the Roswell crash is not only accurate, but was also preceded by the attempts on McCord Air Force Base, could the sightings at Maury Island have been a disoriented Kamikaze pilot looking for the base? The McCord Air Force Base was armed to defend our west coast against further potential attacks after the one made on Pearl Harbor. If the Japanese knew of its existence and purpose, it would have been a feasible target for Kamikaze pilots.

However, the acclaimed sightings were reported over Maury Island located twenty-four miles away. Did they know about the base, but not the exact coordinates? Was the would-be Kamikaze too fatigued to keep his bearings during the flight? Was the potential bomber that far off course due to equipment failure or lack of any navigating system all together? Could he have miscalculated his flight path from not knowing his true starting point having potentially been lost since the Pearl Harbor attack? Might the pilot have had inaccurate intel?

Whether or not the sighting was genuine or a hoax, the story gained new momentum a month later following the Roswell crash. One likely reason for the keen interest in the mysterious "Men In Black" could have been due to the sudden confusion and mistrust in the government and military after the conflicting media reports. Did the public perception of a cover-up renew interests in a possible secret branch of the military involved with shady assignments? Or did the recollection of questionable characters in black suits warning against further mention of the Maury Island events cause the quick back-peddling of the Roswell report to appear even more suspicious?

In any case, speculation about possible connections between the two UFO stories and the growing concerns about government cover-ups inspired new theories about suspicious men in black suits. With the residents of Roswell and much of the general public becoming more convinced not only that MIBs existed, but that they were indeed covert military personal attempting to silence reports of UFOs and other phenomena. Just as with Roswell there is too much speculation around the existence, identities, and purpose of the MIBs to properly cover.

Therefore, I'll offer my thoughts and questions on the subject matter and hopefully introduce some new speculatory paths to explore. Secret groups within the government have been confirmed to exist in the past. When the need arises for a small discrete group of trusted individuals possessing specific backgrounds, skillsets, or insights the U.S. government keeps a tight lid on all persons and happenings related. Even long after one such group has been disbanded and information declassified, it is unlikely the government will be forthcoming with all information. For instance, might the identities of such individuals need to be kept secret for the safety of those individuals?

Are such groups only formed when under very specific and undoubtedly necessary circumstances? Is the formation and concealment of such groups justified in all cases? How can the people feel confident that the answer to both these questions is yes without assurances such as written bylaws or a known and trusted party assigned to enforce such standards? Couldn't covert agencies be formed and fulfill their duties even with the world populace knowing such measures exist when deemed appropriate? See how easy it is was to make a vague declaration of authority without revealing intel to potential enemies?

Governments could disclose the existence of a policy or policies to form specific units, agencies, or temporary branches of government, when necessary, as defined by preset standards agreed upon by a balanced ruling committee. Information such as names, purposes, and type of personal of such groups would remain classified to ensure success and once responsibly able the governments will release the documents and apprise the public.

Would a generic good faith promise to the people compromise the confidentiality of any specific group or objective? If the U.S. Government suddenly made an announcement to the public admitting their occasional formation and use of MIBs on an as needed basis, would the disclosure somehow make the government or the MIBs more vulnerable? Does the government fear that disclosing such information would lead to further distrust?

Is the government trying to uphold national security or just intentionally teasing the public to keep the masses distracted? If there were no conspiracy theories or potential MIB for the populace to focus on, it would be harder to conceal the real information being kept from society.

Is that the entire job of the supposed MIB? To act as a red herring and keep the public eye focused on what could be called the worst kept secrets? Are Roswell, Area 51, and MIB being propagated by the government to keep us from thinking too much about other things? The proverbial smoke in our eyes caused by the government intentionally fanning the flames of popular conspiracy theories keeps us too blind to see the often simpler and more obvious answers.

I'm not suggesting clandestine agencies don't exist within the government and military and I'm sure at least one of those agencies has been charged with investigating UFOs. Don't governments need assigned personnel capable of investigating all reports of unidentified flying objects with a great deal of stealth? Maybe sixty to seventy percent of cases turn out to be a hoax or prank, another ten to twenty percent misidentified pedestrian crafts, another five percent military craft called in by accidental bystanders, three percent undetermined due to lack of evidence or eyewitnesses, but what if that last one percent does turn out to be a known malign enemy aircraft?

If having a classified agency for tediously investigating UFO reports prevents hostile terrestrial craft from carrying out terrorist attacks, hacking and disrupting our systems, stealing information, and potentially igniting a war, they're doing a good and thankless job. Doesn't it make sense to have a secret stealthy team to investigate UFO sightings for potentially enemy craft without alarming the public? Especially if the MIB is actually preventing attacks from those enemy attacks without ever letting the public get wind and therefore also preventing mass panic. In which case, public interest in MIB and entertainment that improves the public opinion of them can be our way of appreciating and supporting the real undercover agency or unit the MIB represents.

Doesn't it make more sense that UFO investigations are more likely done for that purpose than for covering up the existence of aliens? Most of the world's population already believes we're not alone and any secrets pertaining to alien life would more likely be in a lab or an off-world collaborative base that the collective governments of Earth haven't yet disclosed.

Although governments could try harder to earn and retain public trust by at least admitting they do keep secrets and promising to let us in on them when the time comes, sometimes undisclosed investigations are needed to maintain society's sense of security and diplomatic relations with other countries. Is it so bad to think there are superhero-like agents and soldiers keeping the unsuspecting public safe while simultaneously looking snazzy?

On the other hand, let's explore the less favorable possibility that rather than acting as superheroes the MIBs are cleverly controlling information, populations, and even potentially all of humanity. Could they be acting as undercover agents for the various governments of the world to maintain their secrecy and power of the people of Earth? Could they be acting as undercover agents for an extraterrestrial government? Might there be some truth to the theory that the governments of our world are secretly working with an alien government or multiple alien governments?

Scarier still, what if we were already invaded? Could the governments of our planet have already been infiltrated? If an invasion occurred by means of slowly replacing the world leaders of Earth with extraterrestrials, could the MIB have helped to make that happen?

Could their primary job be to debunk information regarding alien life and UFOs in order to prevent people on this planet from openly asking too many questions? Did the MIBs create a complacency within us that there is no extraterrestrial threat and that if there was it would be some obvious attack via a large mothership or by beings who look nothing like us? Are we foolishly making assumptions that if beings from other planets were here, we would know?

Could this also explain why in the last century we have become so technologically advanced so quickly and why governments have become so powerful and controlling? Did they slowly spoon-feed reliance upon technology into the populations as a means of stupefying us? By simplifying our lives has the governments made it easier to control and manipulate us while simultaneously monitoring us through the very devices we've become so dependent on? Have they also decreased brain function by causing the parts of our brains we used to rely on for problem solving and creative thinking to atrophy from lack of use by giving us devices to problem solve and think for us?

Are the MIBs still monitoring us and controlling information? Only now instead of intimidation and media censorship are they using the internet and social media to influence our thoughts and behavior? What if what started as a small secretive agency to investigate UFO reports has since become a much larger global organization whose investigative focus has turned more inward to us, the inhabitants of Earth?

Do they now know more about us than we do? Have they discovered our lost history? If so, could they be keeping it from us in order to maintain our ignorance and their control? What if discovering our past could set us free? If knowledge is power, shouldn't we be relying less on having answers given to us by the internet and more on exploring our planet ourselves?

If the MIB really are a secret group interested in our planet and it's past they wouldn't be the first. Adolf Hitler had a secret group exploring our planet and the histories of ancient cultures. He believed there was power in knowledge and even potential technologies to be discovered. We know that his intentions were not in humanity's best interest. Should we view the MIBs through the same lens? If there are secret organizations interested in Earth's history and past civilizations while the rest of us are preoccupied with space and other planets, why? What's so special about Earth and it's past occupants?

Section Five

Just a Phase

Instead of always looking to the stars for potential threats from beyond, should we be focusing a little more on happenings within our own planet? There is still so much we don't know about our world. We're still learning how to predict and prevent natural disasters, discovering new species with unfathomable abilities we didn't think possible, and pathetically losing battles to common microbes. These are some of the more obvious concerns without better understanding of which have the potential to be problematic for humanity.

Other terrestrial concerns include climate change, over population, depletion of resources, viral mutations and adapted microbials aka 'superbugs' rendering our vaccines and antibiotics ineffective, and human beings. We are a threat to ourselves and to one another, maybe even our own worst enemy. However, these are all considered 'known possible threats' and while some put little to no thought in them, others have just accepted them and have become complacent assuming someone is solving all these problems.

If our own arrogance begets humanity's extinction by one of our known threats, it will likely be our own fault. However, could we be too preoccupied with what might be beyond our planet and so sure we've identified any prospective danger within that we stop trying to understand our immediate surroundings? Are we losing our latent instinct for self-preservation?

We used to be a part of the natural world having internal senses that caused our pulse to quicken when in danger, the hairs on the back of neck to stand and warn us of nearing threats, and our stomach to knot when something unpleasant was about to happen. Shouldn't we have a spiritual connection to our surroundings allowing us to perceive what we can't see, experience moments of clairvoyance, and feel empathy for other living beings whether or not their forms resembled ours? What if by moving further away from the natural world and enveloping ourselves with a vail of technology we are causing our own devolution?

Are we becoming more dependent on our inventions and remembering how to do less on our own? Are we ignoring internal warnings and pushing forward with our latest creations before thorough research and risk assessments can be done? Are we sacrificing basic needs like sleep in favor of indulging in mindless entertainment? How many amazing things did our ancestors know how to do without computers, calculators, or microwaves? How much more did they know about our planet than we do now?

We used to know about monsters, dangerous cave dwellers, and shifting entities because our ancestors warned us. We knew where to find these beings and how to protect ourselves from them because of the explorations of those before us. Have we forgotten or have we convinced ourselves the stories of the past were just myths and overactive imaginations?

Is it easier for us to believe that belligerent aliens with ray guns and impervious suits are going to invade and wipe us out or enslave us? Do we now just blame all paranormal phenomena on travelers from other planets carrying out some secret agenda against us? Did all the spirits, phase shifters, demons, and other hidden beings that were once on this planet with our ancestors just leave?

There was a time when families, even whole societies, openly discussed what they couldn't explain. Have we stopped asking if we're alone on this planet? Might there be ethereal life forms or other entities beyond our perception living on Earth? Can those other entities existing alongside us either beyond our spectrum of perception or in another phase interact with us?

What if our ancestors knew how to use electromagnetism to prevent beings whose molecules vibrate at a different frequency from shifting through our worlds? Could the peoples of the ancient world have known how to manipulate an individual's electromagnetic field using a plethora of methods? Could they fine tune each person's electromagnetic field when it was affected by changes in the Earth's field? How well did they grasp subtle astronomical influences over the Earth's electromagnetic field, their own, and that of other living beings? Are we plagued with stress, migraines, and mental illness more than ancient people were because we lack their understanding of how our electromagnetic fields affect our moods and health?

Theoretically, living entities vibrating at different frequencies could be out of phase with one another. Are there living beings on this planet with whom we're out phase and can't perceive? Can occasional shifts in frequency allow us to sense their presence? Can the frequency at which we vibrate give us a "sixth sense"? Can their electromagnetic fields be affecting ours? Can disruptions in Earth's electromagnetic field alter perception? Can our own frequency and electromagnetic field be altered enough to allow us to shift to alternate phase, move through time, or defy gravity?

If physicists are exploring these questions in their endeavors to acquire theoretical technologies like time travel, could technologically advance survivors of a previous global reset have remained hidden from us for thousands of years by phase shifting? If they are not survivors of an old-world extinction, are they time travelers? Could they be staying hidden to avoid interfering with timelines? Are we their ancient ancestors? Maybe they are waiting to protect us from an impending reset. If we are their past, are they only orchestrating our survival to ensure theirs?

If there are hidden survivors of a previous reset, are they beings living underground and in caves? The people of Hawaii believe their ancestors live and travel through ancient cave systems? Could these cave systems travel through all of what was once Lemuria and connect various cultures throughout the Pacific? Are these tunnels also designed for use of phase shifting technology allowing for travel across vast underwater distances? Could all the ancient gods, spirits, and ancestors the various Polynesian cultures describe be these hidden survivors? Could the Menehune of Hawaii actually be the Akua or descendants of the Akua and could they also be Atua of other Polynesian cultures? Are they really the 'gods' of our ancestors or are they hidden survivors of other resets in our phase who interacted with our ancestors? Could both be true?

If the hidden beings on our planet are survivors from various past resets, are they aware of one another? Do they interact with each other? Do they keep to their own or are they now a collective? Why don't they interact with us? Could Homo Sapiens be out of phase with many other intelligent life forms on this planet? Have they tried to interact with us? Are they waiting for us to evolve further? Are they put off by our nature? Did our ancestors in their fear, greed, or pride do something to the survivors to make them forsake us? Was it our warlike nature? Are they potentially a threat to us?

Maybe it was the hidden people on this planet who disabled the nuclear weapons at the U.S. and Russian bases. If they have been here this whole time, they must have witnessed the bombings of Nagasaki and Hiroshima. This is their planet too. If anything, they were here before us. How might nuclear detonation interact with them in their phase? Are they angry with us for the damage we're doing to the planet we share? Are they trying to protect us from ourselves? Or are they just trying to protect their home from us?

If there are hidden survivors from a reset that occurred due to their own technology, have they learned their lesson? Have they forsaken technology for the comforts of caves? Are they the ones who destroyed and buried ancient monolithic statues all over the world? Were those statues part of the technology? Did they cause a buildup of energy in the Earth's grid? Are the survivors still monitoring the Lay lines for signs of trouble? Could the Lay lines be another unrealized terrestrial threat to current humanity?

Maybe they are not phase shifting survivors, but fragments of residual consciousnesses of previous inhabitants. If the ancient statues all over the world were vessels or servers for containing massive amounts of data indefinitely, could the data intended to be stored have been their consciousnesses? Maybe they knew their end was coming in time to prepare stone vassals for their metaphysical selves. Did it work? Are they existing as spirits or free-floating cognitive energies?

If they are free-floating consciousness, could they be that of previous inhabitants of Earth? Could there be many different consciousnesses of past Earth beings? If there are thoughts and memories of past beings all around us, potentially trying to interact with or influence us, might ancient cultures have referred to these entities as spirits or even gods? Do they use stone constructs to communicate and interact with the physical world?

Maybe once their consciousnesses were transferred to the statues, others buried them to keep them safe. Did some people choose to die rather than transfer their consciousnesses? Were statues only made for important figures of each of the ancient civilization? Was there a lottery? If the statues were buried to protect them, what happened to the consciousness within statues that broke?

The Easter Island Moai were said to have sentience and be able to walk or float themselves to their locations. Is there stored consciousness from previous inhabitants of Earth in some of the Moai? The indigenous people of the island who later were said to have vanished seemed to converse with the Moai as though they were alive. Did the beings within the Moai tell the people of the island how to transfer their consciousness into the Moai? Why were there no bodies? Are the Moai and other statues like them also capable of preserving physical bodies in them? Are there people in stasis in the Moai?

Were other stone creations made for similar use? Is there consciousness stored in the Olmec heads, tikis, totems, and various other monuments? Could they have even been stored in the standing stones of places like Stonehenge and Carnac? What about crystal skulls? Could crystal skulls be housing the collective stored consciousness of entire past civilizations?

If people from a past civilization or civilizations are in stasis within statues and potentially other artifacts all over the planet, why haven't they emerged? Can they emerge? If so, are we unable to perceive them? Are

194

they even trying to communicate with us, or could they be intentionally staying within the stones or in some way out of phase with us to avoid discovery?

Are they waiting for us to reach a technological age closer to what they had? Are they waiting for us to die out? Is there something else coming? Did they emerge from stasis thousands of years ago as the benevolent gods who helped our ancestors? If so when and why did they go back into stasis? If there is something else coming, how do they know? Do they also know what and when? Has it happened before? Will they help us again? Or are they now long gone leaving us to whatever awaits?

The Slave Planet

One strong piece of evidence for The Ancient Astronaut Theory and possible past visitation is the ancient Sumerian tablets containing text that tells their creation story. They described a race of larger, bird-like beings who came to this planet to mine gold. They were the Anunnaki. Apparently, according to some translations, not wanting to exert the time and energy mining the gold themselves, the Anunnaki created humans from clay to mine it for them.

Interestingly enough, there are other ancient creation stories of humans being created from clay or dirt by other worldly beings for manual labor purposes. There are some variations, but essentially humans were created as workers or slaves. Even the various biblical texts have Adam being created to tend the Earth and the garden. He was created to work. In one ancient creation story the Earth was also artificially created out of stone. Recall the Artificial Earth Theory? According to some ancient accounts both the Ancient Astronaut Theory and The Artificial Earth theory could be fairly accurate.

Could the Anunnaki have created the Earth in its very specific location, with its very specific moon resembling basalt spheres, directing very specific comets and asteroids containing very specific elements into the atmosphere? Why would they go through all that trouble? How much trouble is it for them exactly? If they have the technology to create a planet to specification and to direct the space traffic, they probably made it for that purpose which suggest they had time to plan and decide if it was worth it? How desperately might they need that gold? Is it vital for even bigger plans?

Presuming it was the Anunnaki who created Earth, its moon, us and anything else they so desired in the solar system they then preceded to put the Sumerians to work. Writing in any form can describe events and emotions, but tone can change the meaning of words entirely and is often difficult to interpret from text. I, myself am not able to read Sumerian text and must rely on the translations and interpretations of those who can. As of yet, I have not heard the Sumerian text recounted with the negative tone of a people attempting to record atrocities committed against them. Rather, it seems most interpretations convey an affectionate or appreciative regard for the Anunnaki. While others seem to be an objective recording of history.

So it could be said that the Sumerians were happy to know the Anunnaki, revered them as gods, and even learned from some. Some Anunnaki were depicted as teaching the Sumerians and others were not in favor of this. The Anunnaki are said to have come from the twelfth planet in our solar system which has an elliptical orbit. They come to Earth to mine gold when their planet's orbit gets close enough. Scholars, scientists, researchers, and space enthusiasts have not only looked for the planet but have also tried to determine the date of the Anunnaki's next return.

Why are we all in such a hurry for their return? Could the Sumerian text be an accurate account of events? If so, did the Anunnaki create this planet to be a slave planet? Are they responsible for the resets? If they are the ones resetting civilization and are they doing it to cull the population? Or are they doing it not only to counter our evolution, but also to erase our history? Did they fear our potential? Do they hope by keeping knowledge from us they can more easily control us like ignorant cattle?

Did survivors of previous resets remember this history? If there are earlier survivors in stasis within the Easter Island Moai, are they waiting for the next purge by the Anunnaki? Many gods, great prophets, and other religious and/or important figures of the past are said to have left with the promise to return. There are many who believe they will. Human beings seem to be instinctually waiting for someone or something to return. Is it the Anunnaki? Mankind may come to regret the long-awaited reunion.

What if there is no return to be had? What if we are the Anunnaki? Could an ancient ancestor of Earth further along in evolution have visited the newly emerging cultures? Would it have been like people from a sophisticated country visiting a more simplistic one today? Or are the Anunnaki just a part of our complicated genetic makeup?

Perhaps the Anunnaki really did create us. Could they have been the ancient advance people of Earth who dabbled in genetic experimentations? Were they intending to create realistic androids that resembled them in order to do the manual work for them much like we are today? Did they use genetic information collected from several of Earth's hominids in an attempt to create ideal worker traits? Was this a cross cultural joint experiment conducted by many ancestral species?

If Homo Sapien was created through DNA manipulation and designer enhancements, could that explain our genetic potency? Perhaps we are not invasive species from another planet, but invasive unnatural species artificially created on this one through synthetic genes.

Was it their intent to create a less intelligent manual laborer with a shorter life span, but superior capacity to learn? Were some Homo Sapiens also created to specification for the purpose of fulfilling the fantasies and more intimate desires of our creators? We are creating life like androids to specification today for companionship and coital purposes. Could Homo Sapien have started off as something similar?

If we were created and intended to serve our creators, did we at some point gain an unintended and unexpected self-awareness? Did we covet the status and possessions of our creators? Did this create conflict between our creators? Might some have wanted to accept us as sentient beings, while others viewed us as abominations? Were there offspring of the creators and their slaves that were feared or frowned upon? Could it be because they discovered that the artificial DNA of Homo Sapien they created would eventually dominate all others? Was there an attempt to eradicate their mistake? Did this result in war or the great flood as an attempt to rid the Earth of the unnatural genetic code they had created?

Upon discovering their failure at eliminating the aggressive DNA did they abandon this planet? Could those who wanted to intermingle with their synthetic companions have stayed?

Are the Anunnaki one of the already identified human ancestors of Earth? If the others left this planet to avoid being taken over by their inferior artificially created slaves, have they kept an eye on us ever since? Could they be resetting us periodically to contain their mistake to this planet? Is the species of Homo Sapien comparable to the fictional creations known as Cylons in the Television series Battle Star Galactica? Could the idea have come from genetic memory? Do we know somewhere deep down that we are unnatural creations?

Streaming

If consciousness is transferrable and can even be stored in inanimate objects like statues, can it also be shared along a stream? Could the Lay lines actually be streams of collected consciousness or energy by which an entity can transfer its consciousness from one point to another? For example, could a person's stored consciousness in a Moai travel along a Lay line to an Olmec head at will? Could the "spirits" described by ancient cultures have been streams of consciousness traveling between statues and other stone formations along the Lay lines? Ancient people not only used to describe their statues as being able to move and levitate at will, but also as watching over the people of earth. Some ancient people also claimed they communicated with and learned from these statues.

To me, these accounts sound more like they are describing intelligence and freewill than programming or artificial intelligence. Are these statues different containers for consciousness? Can some containers hold consciousnesses of multiple entities? How do those consciousnesses interact with each other? Would they merge into a single collective consciousness and lose who they were, or would they become a collaboration like a council of souls? Does an individual's consciousness need to be stored in physical matter to keep it from merging with a collective consciousness? Can an individual's consciousness choose to merge with or separate from the collective at will? Or can consciousness float around freely as energy? Is that what it means to have

201

free will?

If there are collective consciousness, are those who ascend becoming part of one? Do ascended consciousness get to choose what collective they join? Or is all one universal web? Do beings who choose to store their consciousness in physical matter do so because they don't want to become part of the cosmic connection? Or are there a multitude of collective consciousness? Are there different collective groups or ranks for consciousness to join and potentially ascend through? Do planets have their own networks of consciousness? Does the free will of an individual's consciousness enable choice?

Can a consciousness choose not to share experiences or knowledge gained? Can an individual choose which experiences, feelings, and memories to share with the group and maintain some sort of privacy and independence even while being part of a group? Can it travel from one network to another at will? For example, if a monk from Earth chose to ascend to Earth's collective consciousness, could that monk later ascend to that of the cosmos? If so, can that monk's consciousness traverse through the cosmic collective to descend to another planet's collective and back again at will? Are we still exploring and learning even after we die and/or ascend?

Personally, my one issue with reincarnation has always been my belief that our consciousness is unique and is the primary part of our soul. The spirit may be nothing more than recyclable energy, which once we are done with it can be passed on to a new life. However, our experiences and feelings are our own and in my opinion are what shapes a soul. Do our trials, suffering, and actions in life mean nothing? Is there no justice in death? Are our experiences and consciousness permanent, while our bodies and spirits are only temporary? In that sense, are we all immortal? Is a consciousness and the memories of its own experiences eternal? Or are we nothing? Are we merely frequency and photons flowing in and out of matter from a collective stream to individuals and back to the stream indefinitely?

Could that explain why the universe is expanding? If the universe came into being from the formation of matter and the consciousness imprinted upon that matter, could it have started off tiny and grew as matter and consciousness collected within it? Might the universe have evolved into what we see now the same way seeds grow into Oaks and cells grow into life forms? Or might it have evolved more like a planet forming out of matter caught and collected by a gravitational field? Just as a planet might continue to expand as more matter gets caught in its gravity, gets pulled into the atmosphere, and collects, has the universe been expanding as more memories and experiences are created and collected?

If all of this is true, should we consider streams of consciousness the same way we do data streams? Is consciousness merely a collection of data with matter being the circuitry through which it travels? Is existence just the eternal collecting of matter and streaming of consciousness? Could the Holographic Universe Theory also be at least half right?

If consciousness is a type of data and can be transferred and stored in different types of matter, including stone, can it also be downloaded into a specific format? Could we potentially retrieve an ancient consciousness from a Moai, convert into binary code, and have a computer decipher it? Might consciousness within statues already be stored in binary? Is binary the best numerical sequence for consciousness or is it merely more convenient for the purposes of computing as we know it? Could these stored consciousnesses be responsible for the phenomenon known as crop circles? Could they be trying to alert us to their existence? Are crop circles their way of trying to communicate with us? If so, what are they trying to tell us? Are the geometric patterns of these crop circles meant to show us how to access the information stored in ancient sites? Although most agree that binary would be the ideal form of communication, might there be a more natural code?

If we consider consciousness natural due to it occurring in organic entities, does it follow the Fibonacci pattern? If so, could that be the reason we find so many ancient stones with spiral patterns carved into them? Were those spirals intended to ensure the stone's preservation by using the recognizable pattern to alert future Earth inhabitants that there is a stored consciousness within? We have various signs to warn of dangers such as poison or biohazard which use shapes and images that we consider to be universally recognizable. Will future inhabitants of Earth really be able to decipher their meaning thousands of years after we're gone? If ancient beings were able to relate consciousness to the Fibonacci sequence and expected future intelligences to understand the correlation, did they use spirals as the symbol representing consciousness?

Did ancient beings assume the number sequence that occurs in nature would be recognized by other intelligences similarly to how we assumed intelligences in space would recognize binary communication? If so, were spirals intended for future inhabitants like us, or did Earth's previous inhabitants also hope to communicate with extraterrestrials?

If they were intended for beings from other planets, did they expect these beings to come to Earth? Were they waiting for gods? Or did they hope for entities advanced enough to travel here from another world to have the technology to extract their consciousness from the stones and put them into new bodies?

Maybe the spirals were left for future Earthlings. Could they have been specifically left for us? Do the consciousnesses within stones belong to a race from a previous cycle? Did they communicate through sharing and streaming their thoughts, feelings, and knowledge? Was that how ancient hominids communicated? Did they learn about the resets and wanted to warn future Earth denizens? Or could they have been an advanced ancient civilization still here as our race was emerging? Did they once share the planet with us?

Maybe they were who our ancestors called gods. If we emerged as an ignorant race or genetic experiment gone awry with a propensity for violence, did we pose a threat to them? If they intended to continue sharing the planet with us, were they teaching and guiding our ancestors in an attempt to nullify that threat? Could they have also transported other newly emerging races across the planet with the intent to keep them safe from us?

Were they hoping that by giving us knowledge, spiritual practices, and lessons in philosophy and religion they could calm our aggression? Did our pugnacious nature contort their teachings and result in our ancestors misusing the knowledge taught to us? Did their good intentions make us even more dangerous? Even today, whenever we acquire knowledge, it doesn't take us long to apply it to how we might better kill our enemies.

Is that why the gods left? Were we becoming too much of a threat? Were we setting out to conquer others and did it give us a sense of superiority? Were we responsible for genocides? Could this be what happened to some of Earth's early hominids? Did the ancient beings who tried to peacefully coexist with us by teaching us feel responsible for destruction we brought upon the races we sought to eliminate? Did they try to intervene? Did our conceit drive us to challenge our predecessors and possible creators?

Maybe they caused the great flood to remedy their mistake when they realized our warlike nature couldn't be controlled. Was that their last attempt at protecting themselves, and perhaps other existing Earth races, from us? If so, were the other races protected from the flood? Was it intended to wipe us out completely, or did they allow a percentage of us to survive? If they allowed us to survive, was it because their own beliefs and practices were against genocide? Were they hoping the survivors would evolve?

Displaying their power in causing that flood may have given them reason to believe we would be humbled and intimidated enough to learn to control our nature and finally change. Were they still hoping to live alongside us peacefully? How did they feel when they learned that we either couldn't or wouldn't overcome our nature? Were they afraid for themselves and other inhabitants of this world? Were they saddened and remorseful that the lives lost in the flood turned out to be a meaningless sacrifice? Were they disappointed that all their efforts to neutralize the hostility within us failed? If they were angry, was it at themselves for being unable to find a solution? If these predecessors were both wise and empathetic, it is unlikely they would have been angry with us for being unable to overcome our nature. However, had we been simply unwilling they may have felt justified in directing at least some resentment towards us.

If this is the series of events that played out, maybe they realized that they could not continue their civilization on Earth with the new inhabitants. If they had the technology to leave Earth for another planet, could they have promised to return? Maybe there were some among them who hadn't given up on passing their teachings and practices unto us. If they believed we merely needed a few thousand years to evolve, they may have chosen to venture deep enough into space to account for that required time lapse. Are they waiting it out far enough away? Are they the various revered figures in our history who promised to return? Are they monitoring and potentially even abducting us to see how far we've come?

As for those who may have chosen to transfer their consciousness into stone, was it to keep an eye on our evolution? Are they able to stream their consciousness to the others wherever they are in the cosmos? Could they be delivering progress reports? Are they passively watching, or have they made attempts to influence us? Were they guiding us from within Moai? Are we being tested?

Even if they are only observers who don't interact with us, it may still be for the purpose of testing us. They may be waiting to see what we can achieve on our own. Is it only our behavior they want us to get a handle on? Or are they also waiting to see if our cognition and comprehension improves enough to be comparable with theirs? Are they just one race of many who have stored the consciousnesses on our planet?

Will our advancement eventually lead us to do the same thing? Would obtaining the wisdom to transfer our consciousness elevate our race to finally being eligible to communicate with beings beyond time and space and acquire lost knowledge including Earth's complete history? Will we one day be steaming along Ley lines or collective webs of consciousness as easily as we surf the internet?

Living the Dream

All the effort of so many great minds put into trying to define consciousness, all the theories offering potential answers, and all the attempts to quantify and decode it may be inconsequential. If reality came into being simultaneous and tantamount to consciousness, the physical universe and metaphysical universe may be one and the same. We consider tangible to be perceivable by our sense of touch. Anything touchable we refer to as physical. We interchange the word physical with real thus associating the physical universe with reality.

However, reality is established by perception. Perception is not limited only to our sense of touch, but also to our other four senses. We perceive via sound, smell, sight, and taste. Although we associate our senses with specific parts of our body giving them the impression of being physical, the processes occur in our brain. Furthermore, perception encompasses other occurrences for which we have no associated sense or physical component. Do we have more than five senses?

Some have proposed a sixth sense of clairvoyance and relate it to a third eye. Although the third eye is most often interpreted as a metaphor, it still relates to the perception of sight and a physical bodily feature, our eyes. Those who consider the third eye to have a specific bodily location believe that location to be somewhere on or in the head. Various parts of the brain, including the hypothalamus, have been identified as possible physical mechanisms for the third eye.

Many debate the existence of a third eye, whether or not it has a specific location either external or internal, and if there is a particular bodily structure responsible. Also being considered in those discussions is the possibility only a few have this additional sense and that this may be due to a slowly disappearing trait, newly emerging adaptation, specific gene, or mutation. Could there be an organelle somewhere in the bodies of a percentage of homo sapiens like a vestigial tail? Could it be a residual trait of the evolution process or latent DNA from contributions of unknown hominid ancestors? Regardless, the process of perception still occurs in the brain meaning it's all in our heads.

Are there other senses we haven't identified? By further examining other aspects of perception can we identify more senses and their physical correlations? Awareness, memory, dreams, thoughts, hallucinations, and emotions are all considered to be perceived. Is perception just an overused term to describe the components of the metaphysical universe? Why does it seem so difficult for humans to interpret? Why do humans seek out tangibility, measurability, and definability? What are we trying to prove? To whom are we trying to prove it?

Because we have determined reality to be physical, we in turn seek to also make it tangible. If the physical universe and metaphysical universe are synonymous with one another, there is no need to search for tangible explanations of reality. If tangibility is only perceived by touch, why are we trying to apply it to reality? Touch is but one sense. Why should the perception of one sense define reality? Taste, smell, sound, sight are equally definable sensory methods of perceiving. Shouldn't they therefore be equally applied to reality even if they are just in our heads?

We associate the nose to smell, but smell happens in the brain. We associate our tongue to taste, but taste happens in the brain. We associate our ears to sound and our eyes to sight, but both happen in the brain. Most often we associate our hands to touch, but it also happens in the brain. Even the appearance of two entities or objects, which we consider to be physical, touching one another happens in the brain. The sensation of someone or something touching us happens in the brain. All perception seems to happen in the brain.

If identifying reality with the physical universe means also identifying it with tangibility which is perceived by touch, doesn't that in turn identify reality as perceived? Earlier when considering the components of the metaphysical universe we defined them as perceived as well. However, there seem to be far more senses and perceptions associated with the metaphysical universe than the physical. How can this be accurate? The physical universe being tangible has measurable limitations while the metaphysical universe is infinite. We continually seek to quantify aspects of the physical universe although we presume it to also be infinite.

Did definability limit the physical universe? Is the physical universe nothing more than the universe for which human beings quantified through our own invented principles and definitions? We apply definition based on properties. Properties are definitions of measurements. Is the human species incapable of comprehending and accepting that which can't be held, measured, or defined?

The concept of separating the physical and metaphysical universe is a human concept and is conceived out of flawed logic and/or limited comprehension. For

211

all we know various other entities may have very different concepts of the universe with varying degrees of logic and understanding. What does is it mean to understand? Is comprehension just perception?

Did perception begin with the creation of the universe? Or did perception create the universe? If the big bang was actually the beginning of perception, is the universe just collective consciousnesses? If consciousness came into being from frequency causing a slow buildup of energy into a critical mass, is all else merely perception? Could the elements, their sub particles, and matter just be more imagined notions? Are they merely futile attempts to quantify that which is already established as infinite? Is all of reality dreamt by the collective consciousness generated out of the natural frequency of the universe like a cosmic lullaby forming a dream? Could H.P. Lovecraft be half right in his rendition of the cosmos? Is life but a dream?

The Human Condition

Even if we are one day able to find all the answers to existence and consciousness, will those answers also provide an understanding of ourselves? Will we be satisfied with those answers? Will discovering the secrets of the universe reveal some insight into our own nature? What is human nature?

Is "nature" even the right word? It doesn't quite seem to be natural. There is something about humanity that sets us apart from other life forms on Earth. We can explain the reactions, desires, and behaviors of other creatures due to how they interact with their natural surroundings. However, human reactions, desires, and behaviors often seem in contrast to our environments, to other life forms, and even to ourselves. Therefore, can we even call it human "nature"?

If anything, rather than natural could it be conditioned? Have we lost what might have been our nature over time to be replaced with learned responses? If so, what was human nature prior to our conditioning? What factors lead to the unnatural changes in human behavior? How many current human reactions and behaviors are unnatural contradictions?

If current humans are a culmination of past Hominidae, be they from different evolutionary trees, previous resets, or alien influence, could we be a combination of conflicting natures? Could conquering and interbreeding with other beings in our distant past have resulted in subtle influences over our early design?

It's believed that it's biological to be attracted to our own kind. This is the principle behind the assumption that a serial killer's race can be determined by his or her victim preference. One could say this is instinctual and necessary for the progression of a species. It's natural to procreate and the process is driven by biological attraction. So why have humans obsessed over sexual interactions with gods, demons, angels, birds, snakes, and other oddities throughout history?

What possible justification could there be for any physical attraction towards such beings? Is the assumption that nature seeks to preserve wrong? Rather than a species instinctually mating to preserve and pass on its genetic lineage, is there instead an innate desire for the introduction of new genetic information? Could this be due to a need to diversify? Or is there an inherent understanding in all natural beings that the pursuit and introduction of different genes is necessary for adaptation and eventual evolution?

If, however, there does exist a predisposition to breed with our own kind in order to preserve the species, why do some people find themselves attracted to exotic beings? Is there evidence of an evolutionary connection hidden in our genome? Is this the result of interbreeding between a variety of ancient ancestors? Did some ancient genetic contributors share resemblance to the beings in myths described as gods, angels, and demons? Are the stories of sexual encounters between humans and other beings authentic accounts? Or if Homo Sapiens were created in a lab, were specific attributes from several beings other than just hominids chosen in order to create a "better" chimeric species?

Why are we so warlike? Could it be the potency of one ancestral hominid's nature? Was it that ancestor who spread across the globe conquering others and interbreeding with them? Was the potentially inherited belligerence from one ancestor strong enough to overwhelm all other combined natures of the many lineages that went into our creation? Could we be at war with ourselves internally due to a plethora of conflicting ancestral pedigrees?

What if belligerence doesn't even exist in nature? Assuming it's also not the result of genetic tampering in a lab, could it instead have been a conditioned reaction or reactions? Did the encounters of ancient human ancestors trigger fight or flight responses severe enough to cause a habituated reaction to unfamiliar beings? Did ancient conflicts condition our ancestors to be fearful and defensive opposed to inquisitive? If so, were conditioned responses imprinted on their DNA and passed down to offspring like an adaptation?

Do modern humans have an underlying motivation for finding and vilifying differences between one another? Why are we so ready to segregate ourselves with unnecessary labels and condemn one another? Did the natural curiosities ancient hominids might have had about each other result in traumatic interactions? Whether intentional or unintentional, if having been curious about the differences of other comparable beings somehow caused harrowing consequences, was the byproduct inherited fear? Do we intuitively distrust those who are different?

If we are conditioned to be fearful and warlike due to genetic memories of confrontations in the past, perhaps those confrontations were not between our ancient hominid ancestors. Could there have been bigger, much more profound conflicts leaving a deep inherited unease within us? Perhaps the stories shared by some cultures of gods battling in the skies have pretext. Did our ancestors witness devastation?

Could this devastation have been an ancient war between the technologically advanced civilizations of the most recent reset? Did newly emerging humans watch the previous inhabitants of the world destroy one another? Or did survivors of the last reset pass along warnings through recounting their ordeal? Were there really beings from other planets battling in Earth's skies? Or has a single group of alien beings been visiting Earth and resetting humanity? Have we been purposely conditioned to dread the beings who created and enslaved humans?

Could this also be the reason for some of our other bizarre obsessions? Could our desire for knowledge, freewill, and traveling through constellations all stem from our memory of having been created as slaves by a race of beings from the stars? Might this also explain our arrogance and desire to be godlike? Does our warlike response to perceived threats come from a deep seeded defiance? Did our ancestors rebel against enslavement and strive for the freedom to escape into the cosmos?

One constant among humanity that even transcends time is our freewill. Is this just our truest nature stronger than any conditioned responses? Or does it stem from a developed defiance? Is defiance the result of an ancient traumatic and infuriating memory, such as slavery, and our desire to never again endure what transpired in the pasts? Is that defiance also responsible for our aggression? Or were we the original aggressors? Could defiance be a necessary perpetuator of freewill?

Is what we call "will" another perceived sense? Or is it more closely related to spirit? Can humans learn to strengthen and utilize their will? Could that be the source of our inner power to survive, heal, and sometimes even muster seemingly impossible strength? We normally attribute that to adrenaline, again attempting to find a tangible explanation and quantify it, but what if we're drawing upon another source of energy? Could human will be developed and/or converted into some type of harnessable power? If so, what benefits might there be? What potential problems might arise from tampering with human will?

By strengthening will power, can a person become resistant to temptations, emotions, and specific sensations like pain for instance? This concept is accepted and practiced by many. If strengthening our will helps us to overcome weaknesses and character flaws, can it also negate certain behavioral aspects of human nature or potential conditioning? Can a person's strengthened will coerce another? If so, could ancient hominids with stronger wills have contributed to modern humans more than other hominids? Could some beings have mastered controlling and manipulating their own will and potentially even that of others?

In what ways could a strengthened will be utilized? Does it become a force we can use on others? Can one individual inflict will upon another? Can it be transferred or shared between one another, like streaming consciousness? If so, for what purpose and could there be profound consequences?

Interactions between various organisms likely leaves lasting effects and can potentially cause any number of alterations to those organisms including their perceptions. The interactions between communal species influences a range of social attributes. Could the potent enough will of one individual manipulate an entire group? Psychologists refer to the ability of one person's emotions to spread through and instigate a group as herd mentality. Could someone with a strong enough will deliberately enforce it upon others thereby potentially controlling an entire population?

What affects can the assertion of another's will have on the behaviors and personalities of other? Are there lasting side effects from exposure to the intense willpower of another? Might perceptions be distorted enough to cause metaphysical harm? Could the psychological phenomenon known as "shared psychosis" be the result of one severe will dominating another? Has a history of humans exerting their wills recklessly and even destructively against each other caused irreversible distortion of our nature?

What if early humans had the will of a powerful entity or entities forced upon them? Were ancient hominids enslaved by "God's will" or "the will of the gods"? Were early humans manipulated through omnipotence? If so, would such an affliction have dire repercussions not only for humanity, but also for the subjugator or subjugators? Could remnants of a binding will remain within us provoking defiance, thus freewill? Is what we consider human nature simply an unnatural volition?

The Missing Chapters of Humanity

Instead of being created, either by past beings intending us to be slave labor or attempting to artificially evolve themselves through genetic manipulation, what if we accidently created ourselves? Could residual radiation from ancient nuclear conflicts have resulted in the mutation leading to Homo Sapien development and evolution? Could ancient technologies have caused subtle changes on the molecular level resulting in a slow, but eventual emergence of the new hominid species? If so, was it due to the effects of the energies used in ancient technologies such as frequency, electromagnetism, and photonics?

If we did accidently create ourselves and not because one or more of our hominid ancestors was intelligent enough to have had a technological mishap, could it really have just been happenstance? Could the consumption of a specific compound have altered the DNA of a previous hominid? Did ingesting the compound give that hominid an intellectual boost? There are various compounds which do have profound effects on our brain chemistries. Did one of the ancient species haphazardly ingest a plant or fruit that coincidentally contained some brain altering compound?

If so, then could the alteration of that hominid's brain chemistry have then been passed down to, and perhaps even more pronounced in, the hominid's offspring? Could such changes in brain chemistry be exacerbated by interbreeding? For example, if a Neandertal initially consumed a substance which altered his or her brain chemistry and then produced a child with another hominid such as Homo Erectus, could that child have possessed altered DNA? If so, could that altered DNA have continued to change with each new generation? What if new generations continued consuming the plant or fruit containing the substance? What if the various hominids also continued to interbreed? What if they also interbred with other hominids like Denisovans, Homo Habilis, and Homo Heidelbergensis?

Could all of the past hominids have been far more intelligent than we believe? Did each of the ancient hominids have their own cities and cultures? If their intellectual development was just inadvertent evolution due to continual introduction of new genetic information from several sources such as consumption, interbreeding and additional genetic information entering Earth from space, could more potent changes have been intentionally introduced later on by one or more of our ancestors? Did one of them perhaps realize that consuming a specific fruit or flower produced a desired effect? We intentionally use, and in some cases misuse, specific substances now in order to alter our own brain chemistry.

Could some of the ancient alchemic concoctions of our more recent history have been conceived from genetic memories of mixtures created and consumed by ancient hominids? Did use of those mixtures contribute to the adaptations of those hominids and the eventual emergence of Homo Sapiens? Might some of the medicinal compounds we use today have already been in use in our distant past? Could ancient hominids have been consuming certain herbs and roots in order to combat specific illnesses? If so, could that have altered the genetic information within the microbes responsible for those illness enough to create new variations of those microbes?

Did new strains of viruses develop from interbreeding and consuming specific substances? Did those viruses in turn further change the genetic information in the cells of certain ancestral hominids? Likewise, if not an accidentally ingested chemical compound from a food source, could there have been a particular microorganism in the water? What combination of changes and in what order could account for such dominant DNA that might have caused the diverse collection of hominids on Earth to dwindle down to only Homo Sapien?

What if the other hominids didn't all die out or slowly integrate into modern Homo Sapien? What if some did go underground or left the planet all together? Could one or more of the ancient species still be thriving somewhere on our planet, or even beyond?

If some of the ancient hominids left the planet, taking their culture and knowledge with them, could they still be out there? Could we find evidence of their interplanetary journey on neighboring planets as we venture further out into space? Could there be structures and information left behind for us to follow? Are they still sending messages in an attempt to communicate?

As for those who stayed behind, might they have intentionally tampered with the DNA of their own offspring in order to increase their chances of survival? If a previous nuclear war altered the Earth's atmosphere enough to prevent complete restoration even by the best technology our advance ancestors may have had, could they have realized that the new conditions of the planet were not ideal for the development of future generations? Could they have added genetic information to Homo Sapien DNA in order to improve our quality of life and longevity?

Hypothetically, if a nuclear war did take place and destroy the previous cultures of Earth and the pyramids were built as atmospheric restoration structures, perhaps they had their limits. Could the scientists left behind to clean up the damage and make the planet habitable again have realized that they couldn't completely undo the damage? Did they conclude that even with their best technology and global effort it would still take hundreds, thousands, or even millions of years for the damage caused by nuclear fallout and waste to dissipate? If so, could altering the DNA of future Homo Sapiens have been their way of leaving behind a legacy? Is that the reason for why only Homo Sapiens survived? Were we the only species genetically altered to survive on a potentially radioactive Earth?

Or was Homo Sapien DNA the only one capable of surviving? Could all other advance hominid species have left Earth leaving behind a group of scientists primarily consisting of Homo Sapiens? Could the Neanderthal and Denisovan DNA found in the Human Genome have come from their representatives that stayed behind? As new generations emerged with more and more of the Homo Sapien contribution as well as more exposure to residual radiation did Homo Sapien DNA gain potency?

What if instead of a group staying behind to clean up the planet, the structures were built as self-sustaining for the amount of time calculated to render the Earth habitable again? Did a group come back once that time had been reached? Did previous inhabitants leave behind a satellite to monitor the atmosphere to know when it would be safe to return? Could we really be the offspring of ancient astronauts? Perhaps they only left the planet long enough to wait it out in space, but never reached a new habitable planet. Could living in space for an extended period of time have altered their DNA? Were Homo Sapiens the only hominids who survived the presumably long years in orbit?

Could this also explain why our bodies don't seem to be designed for moving, living, and continued evolution on this planet? We're all in physical and emotional pain. Our bodies seem to deteriorate early on in our life cycles. We accumulate wear and tear experiencing joint and back complications before we've fully developed into adults. If our bodies have not completely matured until our mid-twenties to early-thirties, why are we afflicted by arthritis, hearing loss, vision loss, and various other seemingly age-related ailments by our mid-teens?

Why do we also seem to suffer from chemical and hormonal imbalances as well as mental illnesses? Is the gravity of Earth too severe upon our bodies? Do the various electromagnetic fields and frequencies of the planet impact our bodies ability to maintain proper hormonal balance, biochemistry, and brain waves? If so, could this be the result of generations of human ancestry developing in space? Could this also be why our current life spans are much shorter than those reported by the mythologies and historical records of ancient cultures?

If our ancestors did have floating cities and antigravity vehicles, could the technology used to keep them airborne have prolonged the lives of past hominids? If the cities required specific planetary conditions to stay afloat, perhaps those conditions were also ideal for sustaining human life. Assuming colder temperatures were required to keep the cities afloat and/or the technology was simply made possible due to the planetary conditions of the ice age, the colder climate might have coincidently resulted in longer life spans. If an ancient nuclear conflict really is responsible for our lost history and for altering both our planet and DNA, could it have had even more profound changes? Could it have increased Earth's gravity or changed the electromagnetism and/or frequency of the planet?

What if there was no nuclear war? What if the Earth was already a violent place with ever shifting magnetic fields, ever fluctuating gravity, and a nearly constant bombardment of additional forces and material raining down from space? If a wide variety of life still managed to evolve and thrive in all that chaos, could the intelligent life forms have conspired to stabilize the Earth? If resets are just a natural occurrence as part of the great cyclical nature of the universe, then perhaps the awareness of the various hominids lead to an understanding and potential fear of mass extinction. If so, could their intelligence have also made them arrogant? Did they think they could put an end to the eternal universal cycle by creating a moon and an artificial atmosphere to stabilize and protect Earth? What if in doing so, they were actually more detrimental to life than helpful?

Did the ancients realize their mistake only after it was too late to undo it? Did they make attempts to fix it? Did they create technologies to compensate for the changes that would have occurred on Earth from creating a moon and/or adding magnetosphere? Could that be the purpose behind some of the ancient creations? Were they attempting to harness and direct the energies they had created or altered?

What if instead of creating the ancient structures as a means to balance out whatever they may altered by creating a moon, they already had these structures in place? If these structures were ancient water treatment plants, power plants, computers, or any other device requiring specific energy could the placement of the moon have backfired either by overloading these structures with energy or depleting them? If the moon had too profound of an effect on the magnetic fields surrounding these structures, could this be the reason for why so many ancient cultures seemed to have buried their creations?

Perhaps the ancient creations were buried simply to keep them safe. If entire cultures did leave the planet with the intent to return one day, could they have buried their larger creations for safe keeping? Could the structures have been buried by other cultures after conflicts? Did new religious beliefs emerge which caused the people of the time to bury their past? Did an advance race of ancient astronauts bury the evidence of their presence here? How many of History's lost chapters still remain buried within our mysterious planet?

The Last Chapter of Humanity

Earlier I asked if our memories, feelings, and experiences meant nothing. However, if they do contribute to our soul and possibly even the collective, could we be building upon the universe in a profound way? My writing, drawings, and paintings were bettered over the years by my pain. My experiences enriched my creations and gave them a power of their own that others can feel. Could we be gaining power and enriching our creations with it?

Could our pain and experiences build up as energy within us that we are able to transfer into our creations and imprint a sort of spirit upon them? Is that why some monolithic creations seem alive? Could we one day extract the knowledge, feelings, and memories imprinted upon the ancient creations?

Likewise, will we eventually be able to consciously access the knowledge and experiences of the distant past safeguarded within our genetic memory? If we could identify tangible attributes of our genome that store the genetic memory of our ancestry, could we stimulate or manipulate those aspects into bringing those memories forward from the subconscious to the conscious? Could we potentially even use a sort of projection or modern 3d printing technology and computers to render genetic memory viewable? For example, if we determine the tangible attributes responsible for memory to be physical microtubules could we replicate the structures and patterns of those microtu-

226

bules and transfer or copy the information from our brains to the replicas? Could we then convert the information into binary to be processed by computers?

The single celled slime mold scientifically named Physarum polycephalum has been found to have a matrix of cytoplasmic microtubules which in more recent studies seem to demonstrate an ability to retain information. This suggests awareness and memory. If that's all that's required to imprint information such as experience and memory upon a physical plane is microtubules, then could we create an artificial canvas for storing metaphysical data such as awareness, memory, and emotion? Could this organism be proof of a tangible requirement for consciousness and memory?

Or can such metaphysical information also be stored on matter without microtubules? Could we merely be looking at an example of Panpsychism that also just so happens to be a living organism with microtubules? Perhaps one day we will be able to extract ancient memories from stone? Might the minerals and microstructure of stone provide similar conditions to that of microtubules for storing and transferring information? Microtubules are polar with their protofilaments aligned to the same orientation providing a sort of directional flow. Could we consider the crystalline structures of minerals and the strata of stones to be doing the same thing? If information is transmitted throughout an organism via electric impulse traveling through microtubules, could the piezoelectric properties of crystalline structures provide low but continual electric stimulation suitable for maintaining metaphysical information? Perhaps there's even more metaphysical information stored on and within the ancient megalithic structures than there is within our DNA.

If memory can be imprinted and transferred like

computer data, can false memories be intentionally created and planted? Could existing memories be modified
into false ones? Might someone have modified or created information to rewrite existing stored memories
similar to how computer code can be used to create viruses and other malware? If such a thing occurred and
the modified memories were imprinted onto our DNA
and passed along, how might it have changed us?
Could it be used to manipulate us? Could it be preventing us from accessing certain stored memories? Was it
done out of malice or to protect us from a traumatic
history? If we are merely lifelike androids created from
synthetic DNA, might that DNA have also contained
synthetic memory? Could the genetic memory we contain and pass on be limited due to it having been written by our creator or creators? Could our genetic
memory be nothing more than ancient artificial intelligence?

Even if genetic memory is being passed along in
DNA, could it only be passed along in specific genomes?
What if the reason we cannot consciously access genetic
memory is because Homo Sapien DNA is artificial?
Could genetic memory only be passed along in the latent, but natural DNA of the past hominids of which
we're comprised? If Homo Sapiens really were created
by ancient hominids using DNA samples from each
hominid as well as lab created synthetic DNA, could the
reason why our subconscious can only occasionally access inherited memories be because the synthetic DNA
was essentially a blank slate? If Homo Sapien DNA is
synthetic and potent enough to override all other ancestral genomes, do we only possess a portion of our ancestors memories within us?

If Homo Sapien DNA was artificially created and we
are essentially androids, are we capable of eventually

becoming part of the natural world as we interact with it? Could the potency of the synthetic DNA lessen over time and allow for eventual reemergence of the natural DNA from previous Earth inhabitants? Will we evolve into a single new natural Earth hominid, or will we split into several separate species? Will we see the androids we're creating now also become more natural and eventually evolve into something like our current selves?

If we are able to download ancient experiences in the future, could we also share them with our android creations? Would they then also pass the information down to their offspring? What if they eventually become natural enough to consider themselves an evolved species of Earth, but forget how they came to be in the first place? If androids possess computer brains with a limited capacity compared to a natural brain, will they have to overwrite information as time passes making them forget their very beginning? Sound familiar?

If Homo Sapiens were created thousands of years ago, did we forget because we had artificial brains? Is our creation of pseudo-humans just history repeating itself? Has it happened before? If so, did it happen on Earth? Or could Homo Sapien DNA have actually been created elsewhere in the universe and simply found its way to Earth by happenstance? Could Homo Sapiens be a plague of artificial replicators spreading across the cosmos destroying naturally occurring life forms like something out of a science-fiction story?

If Homo Sapien DNA did originate elsewhere and we are an invasive species, could our DNA have actually hindered intelligence rather than progressed it? The Earth ancients seemed to have possessed far more knowledge and understanding of the planet and the cosmos. They also may have had superior technologies which used natural energies, caused limited or no damage to the planet, and left no trace behind for us to reverse engineer.

However, we create technology through destruction of natural resources, cause harm to the planet, and amass hordes of garbage and toxic waste. We litter the planet and even the solar system and consider it an unfortunate part of technological advancement. What if it's not advancement at all? What if we are actually devolving?

The more technology we create the more we become dependent upon it. We are forgetting how to do the simplest things without the aid of computers and search engines. We are relying upon readily available data that has been uploaded instead of committing information to memory. We are not learning if we are not forming new memories. Memory creates new neurological pathways in the brain and keeps it stimulated. Technology dependency atrophies the brain. The blue light from screen has been shown to damage cells and disrupt brain chemistry and the natural circadian rhythm. Our lives have also become so comfortably melded with technology that we have removed ourselves from the natural world and may be gradually losing our natural instincts and abilities.

This is just what we have done to ourselves through what we perceive as advancement. What if it's all merely the ill-inevitable continued deterioration of humanity from a singular event? Could the introduction of Homo Sapien DNA into the hominid gene pool have halted any further progression of the various Earth Hominidae family? If the DNA was that of an invasive species and/or artificial design and its potency resulted in all the bottle neck of human evolution down to just us, could it have also gradually stupefied the progression of intelligent evolution? Was the emergence of

Homo Sapien the beginning of the next reset?

If the DNA is an unnatural product of directed gene sequencing lab synthesizing in order to create an ideal being, might it explain our comfort with and desire for binary technologies? Could it also explain our fears of many of the natural world's attributes? Why do we flee from insects? Why are we so uncomfortable outside? Why do we seem to need to separate ourselves from nature? Could it be because Earth's natural environment is foreign to us? Do we fit in better with computers and silicon than we do rocks and soil?

Is our supposed evolution actually leading us down a path of limited capability? Are we slowly becoming less life like and more machine like? Is it because our ancestors were infected with Homo Sapien DNA? Was it just accidental happenstance? Did a curious advanced race of beings from another planet send self-replicating androids, capable of interbreeding with Earth's various hominids, to explore the cosmos? Did one of Earth's ancient civilizations create custom slaves and/or sex robots? Was Homo Sapien DNA sent here specifically to infect the natural inhabitants of Earth like some sort of computer virus with the intent to rewrite genetic code?

Regardless of the Homo Sapien origins, could our DNA actually be making us stupider? Now that we've dwindled down to one species, removed ourselves from nature, destroyed ancient texts and artifacts through war and religious purges, over populated to the point of mental instability and physical unsustainability, and become dependent on computers have we reached the end of our cycle? Have we run out of history to repeat and need to start over?

What if the other hominids didn't succumb to a reset, hybridize with Homo Sapien, or go extinct? If they did leave the planet or go into hiding, might they be significantly more evolved by now? Could they have acquired certain desired natural attributes, like camouflage or regeneration, that we see in aquatic and insect species? If they continued to embrace the natural world and deepen their understanding and relationship with it, could they have undergone a true evolution? Are they now able to live under water? Did they become the beings known as Naga, Kapa, and Merfolk? Did the branches of the Hominidae tree split into those who would become apes, those who would become modern humans, and those who would become something even more intelligent and with greater abilities and evolutionary potential?

Could it be because some hominids chose to hide and climb trees, some chose to use tools and change their environment, and others chose to communicate with, imitate, and bond with other species and their natural environments? Did those who continued to hide and climb trees remain stuck as apes in their refusal to change or adapt? Did those who rejected their natural environment and changed it in such a way that continuously removed them from natural environments and other species become humans? Did those who observed their natural environment and imitated other organisms around them develop into a greater species?

If one or more ancient advance race did leave the planet a long time ago, could they be responsible for the abduction phenomenon? Earlier I theorized that perhaps as Homo Sapien evolved other more advanced hominids may have still been here and could have been the beings referred to as gods. If they are those beings and did leave Earth with the promise to return like so many ancient texts say, then could they be the ones responsible for some reported abductions? If they returned to see what Homo Sapiens became and where we are heading, could they be trying to fix our DNA?

Another possibility is that they are simply abducting individuals with enough latent DNA of past hominid species, like Neanderthal, to extract a complete genome of that species from the individual's DNA in order to preserve it. Might they be harvesting and, in a sense, rescuing the genomes of previous Earthlings? Might they be trying to undo the eradication of the other hominids, especially if they feel responsible for it? Could they be intending to reset the planet themselves? Are they attempting to rid the Earth of Homo Sapien once and for all? Or are they simply looking for a way to alter the invasive DNA so that it's better suited for Earth's environment, less devastating to the planet and other organisms, and capable of natural evolution into something other than a machine?

Perhaps once Homo Sapien DNA is modified enough we will see the previous humanoid species reintroduced. If the Homo Sapien DNA potency problem is fixed, could we once again interbreed with the other various hominids to create true hybrids without the bottle neck effect and potentially evolve together into a vast variety of beings? Could we have a planet filled with Merfolk, Fairies, Vampires, Shapeshifters, Naga, Tengu, giants, elves, and so much more?

Humanity's Epilogue

There are accounts of the world actually being full of different beings before the flood. The great flood is not merely a Biblical mythos or even the first of its kind but can be found in nearly every culture including the earliest known. Some suggest that these ancient stories are a way for early humans to attempt to justify a devastating natural event. Many theories as to exactly what kind of natural event and when it occurred have been proposed. Others disagree and argue that it was an intended, intelligently designed planetary cleansing. Again, there again numerous suggestions as to when and who or what may have orchestrated it.

If the planet was at one time laced with an eclectic assortment of intelligent species and civilizations and the great flood not only occurred but was a directed cleansing, should we consider it a mass genocide event in which all intelligences on Earth were exterminated except for Homo Sapiens? If so, what does that say about our lineage? Were we the culprits? Did our ancestors commit mass genocide to ensure we would be the only race remaining? Have we been tyrannical, arrogant, and belligerent since our very inception? Are we a parasitical plague upon the planet and all other life forms?

Despite what we may think of ourselves, humans may not be the only intelligent life left on the planet. Our perceptions are so limited that most human beings cannot see the equal and even greater intelligences right before their eyes. Is it our arrogance that perpetuates the belief that we alone are capable of complex thinking? Or is it derived from a lack of observation? When our eyes are open and witness to other creatures thinking and solving problems, is it a lack of understanding that leads us to conclude it must be a fluke or they are only copying us without knowing what they're doing? Why are we so hubris, blind, and obstinate?

The vast and diverse assembly of life forms on this planet display an array of abilities far beyond our own and all of them seem to possess the basic understandings of the natural world. Not only do other life forms display evidence of being able to predict the weather right down to subtle changes in pressure, but they also seem to sense changes beyond our atmosphere whether they notably impact the planet or not. This suggests that not only are those basic natural instincts tuned to the planet, but to the entire cosmos as well.

Furthermore, we have witnessed many different animals prepare for these changes, react to their environments in complex and unexpected ways, and display an ability to problem solve by physically changing their environment or items in their environment even occasionally through the cooperation with other species or the use of other species or tools. We have even witnessed animals using tools for fun or playing with interesting objects. Other creatures do all this without destroying their environments.

Meanwhile human beings are unable to survive on our own out in the natural world, alter our environments by destruction and pollution, and live in our filth. Our reality is minimal not only due to our limited spectrum of perception, but also due to our own narrow-mindedness. We are unable or unwilling to entertain the notion that we are not superior beings, not even on this planet. We continue to close our eyes and minds to the natural world and the knowledge of the ancient past and favor burying our heads in the potentially detrimental technologies we've produced.

We are, however, constantly singing about ancient forgotten knowledge, writing it in our stories, and displaying it in our art both consciously and unconsciously. We are captivated by stories of suffering and triumph. Is there a genetic memory within us trying to warn us about our forgotten history through the means of inspiration and imagination? Did we already go down this path before or are we the product of other technological civilizations' mistakes? Or could it be a false memory encoded onto our DNA to keep us fixated on questionable obsessions such as superiority, technological advancement, body modification, immortality, and control? Did there need to be a lie to keep us motivated towards endeavors that would distract us and thereby prevent us from uncovering the truth of our existence? Perhaps the lie is the promise of a better life through technology.

It could be that the scenario described in Aldous Huxley's Brave New World has already come to pass. If Homo Sapien is the result of biological experimentation in the past, could we have been engineered to consider ourselves superior in order to prevent us from doubting ourselves and to elicit contentment and compliance from us? Especially if we were created as slaves, might we have been designed to believe ourselves special? What if in all actually we are the lowest ranking class and simply aren't aware of it? Perhaps previous Earth races did create us as compliant slaves happy to worship and make offerings to the gods, but once they left the planet, they had no need for such ignorant, inadequate low beings so they left us here like discarded machines.

Might there even be some truth to the notion that we are something akin to cattle? If we are an artificial creation designed to serve a higher intelligence, could we have been deliberately made too ignorant to properly evolve? Do our bodies serve a specific purpose? Could our brains have been manufactured to operate at only a limited capacity in order to allow another consciousness to inhabit our bodies when necessary? Are we merely spare bodies for harvest preserved by having just enough consciousness to keep an electrical flow throughout?

Were we also made destructive in order to keep our numbers manageable? If the reason for our creation as slave labor is to mine precious metals as some have suggested, could we have also been genetically manipulated to be materialistic and greedy? Could we have been designed to covet those metals to keep us mining them?

If we were manufactured, what if it wasn't to be slaves, companions, or replacement bodies? Could Homo Sapiens have been made as biological weapons? If we have been belligerent since inception, could it be part of our intended programming? Might we have been created by one race to destroy another? Did it backfire on our creators? Were they unable to temper and control their own creation? Do we have design flaws within us which make us prone to be ravenous, distrustful of others, and unable to coexist with anyone including ourselves? We make robots for weapon and war purposes. Are we just repeating the story of our own creation? If so, are we doomed to suffer the same fate as our creators?

Unfortunately, it seems that no one wants to learn our history. Anything we discover about ourselves that we don't like we bury, erase, or destroy. Isn't it better to accept new discoveries and to try to learn about ourselves so that we can improve ourselves and avoid making the same mistakes as our ancestors? Even if we should discover that all of the unfavorable possibilities I've suggested up to this point are true and we are nothing more than invasive, unnatural, destructive, machines, shouldn't we want to know so that we can take measures to at least try to correct our flaws? The truth may hurt, but it may only be one truth of many.

What if all we currently perceive is merely a fraction of what actually exists and there is an expanded reality awaiting us should we allow our minds to connect, or possibly reconnect, to it? Perhaps all the answers are there, but personally I prefer questions. Answers feel like the end while questions open up channels to new concepts and exploration. Answers lead to acceptance which becomes complacency. Questions inspire further exploration and new discoveries. It is disappointing to say the least when I hear someone say that we have discovered all there is to discover, created all there is to create, or done all there is to do. I believe those sentiments to be impossibilities despite my belief that nothing is impossible.

Has so much of the populace lost their curiosity, interest, and enjoyment in our world? Have we truly reached a plateau in our development such that we rather maintain a structured life dictated by inconsequential societal values such as monetary and material gains to sit and wallow in? What if all we need to do to reclaim our lost history and rediscover the knowledge of the ancients is to unplug?

We live in the information age, but are we truly informed? We think with all our advanced technology and the world wide web we have all the power and knowledge, but knowledge is power and if all the information available to us is false where does that leave us? It's easy for people to forget that the information on the world wide web had to be added by other people. Yet we are so quick to seek answers from the web as though it were an all-knowing entity instead of exploring all the possibilities and finding our own answers. Does this make us vulnerable to manipulation?

Have we become gullible to the overflow of false information and ignorant to our own cognitive decline due to our dependence and apparent addiction to the instant gratification the web offers? Is our natural empathy also being bombarded with the toxic emotions others spew carelessly into the cyberverse without regard for the impact such negativity can have on one another? Has the increased use and dependence of the internet cause humanity to become stupider, apathetic, impatient, and even more demanding, ravenous and hubris than we already were? Are we now approaching the end of our cycle?

About the Author

Anastasia is a Japanese American who grew up in foster care but managed to become part of the 1.8% of foster children to graduate from a university. She speaks Japanese as well as a broken mix of French, English, German, and a bit of Hebrew. As young as three years old she was interested in a multitude of subjects, reading on an adult level, and writing theories and stories of her own. Anastasia simultaneously pursued degrees and certifications in Veterinary Medicine, Chemical Engineering, Pathology, Genetics, Psychology, Philosophy, and Graphic Design. Known online as Alien Anatomy, Anastasia has a blog for theories that didn't make it into her books. When asked about her many passions she replies, "I was told I would amount to nothing, believed I could do anything, and decided to do everything".

Follow the author

www.thehistoricalfictioncompany.com/hp-authors/
anastasia-martin

www.historiumpress.com

www.ingramcontent.com/pod-product-compliance
Lightning Source LLC
Chambersburg PA
CBHW051004140626
46546CB00016B/329